HERO

UNLEASHING GOD'S POWER
IN A
MAN'S HEART

DERWIN L. GRAY

Hero: Unleashing God's Power in a Man's Heart
© 2009 by Derwin L. Gray

ISBN 978-1-935416-22-7

Cover and interior design by Gearbox.

Published by Summerside Press, Inc., 11024 Quebec Circle, Bloomington, Minnesota 55438 www.summersidepress.com.

Summerside Press™ is an inspirational publisher offering fresh, irresistible books to uplift the heart and delight the mind.

Printed in Canada

DEDICATION

I dedicate Hero to my bride and queen, Vicki. More than any other person on earth, you have inspired me to live a heroic life because I have experienced the passion and depth of your heroic life.

To my daughter, Presley. From the very first moment I saw your beautiful brown eyes, you captured my heart. You are a great leader and one of my best friends. Thanks for being my "wingman" on road trips to preach.

To my son, Jeremiah "Big Bull" Gray. I have no doubt that you will be ten times the man I am. I am honored to be your father, son.

To "theGathering," the church where I am pastor of preaching and spiritual formation: May this book inspire us to be a community of heroes.

And most of all, I dedicate *Hero* to the Great Hero. When I was lost on the freeway of life, You said, "Follow Me; I AM the way home." When my mind was captured by lies, You said, "Listen to Me; I AM the Truth." And when I was lifeless, You said, "I AM the Life; embrace It and live." My heart is filled with adoration and appreciation. Thank You.

Special thanks goes out to Alan Bacon, my first mentor, Dr. Norm Geisler, Dr. Barry Leventhal, and also Dr. Ken Boa who has mentored me from afar. I am grateful to Chris McGinn for her proofing and keen insights. And to Barbara Farmer, you made the editing process fun. Thanks for believing in me enough to recommend me to the great team at Summerside Press.

CONTENTS

A Special Note vii

Introduction ix

SECTION ONE—THE UPWARD JOURNEY

Entry 1: The Great Hero Is the Great Creator.................................... 1

Entry 2: The Great Hero Is Our Great Father 7

Entry 3: The Great Hero Wants to Know You Face-to-Face 11

Entry 4: The Great Hero Is Our Great Protector 15

Entry 5: The Great Hero Is the God of Integrity.............................. 19

Entry 6: The Great Hero Is in Control... 23

Entry 7: The Great Hero Is Faithful 27

Entry 8: The Great Hero Has Always Been the Great Hero 31

Entry 9: The Great Hero Is Great in Wisdom.................................... 35

Entry 10: The Great Hero Is Love 39

Entry 11: The Great Hero Is the Great "I AM".................................. 45

SECTION TWO—THE INWARD JOURNEY

Entry 12: Hero, Where Are You?... 53

Entry 13: Hero, Discover Your True Self in the Wilderness 57

Entry 14: Hero, You Are Alive 61

Entry 15: Hero, You Are Wearing a New Suit.................................... 65

Entry 16: Hero, God Killed His Son to Be Your Friend........................ 69

Entry 17: Hero, You Are Not Who You Used to Be 75

Entry 18: Hero, God Is Not Mad at You 81

Entry 19: Hero, You Are No Longer a Slave...................................... 85

Entry 20: Hero, You Have a Father Who Runs................................... 89

Entry 21: Hero, You Are a Branch 97

Entry 22: Hero, You Are a Disciple 103

Entry 23: Hero, You Are God's Athlete, Part I...................................107

Entry 24: Hero, You Are God's Athlete, Part II..................................111

Entry 25: Hero, Jesus Teaches You How to Pray................................117

SECTION THREE—THE OUTWARD JOURNEY

Entry 26: Hero, Embrace the Great Story 125

Entry 27: Hero, You Are the *Ecclesia*..131

Entry 28: Hero, You Are Valuable to the *Ecclesia*..............................137

Entry 29: Hero, Love Your Wife with a Jesus Kind of Love, Part I 143

Entry 30: Hero, Love Your Wife with a Jesus Kind of Love, Part II 147

Entry 31: Hero, Husbands Need a Jesus Kind of Respect...................153

Entry 32: Hero, Parenting Matters to God 159

Entry 33: Hero, There Is Heroic Single Living 165

Entry 34: Hero, Pursue the True Treasure, Part I 169

Entry 35: Hero, Pursue the True Treasure, Part II 175

Entry 36: Hero, Work Heroically..181

Entry 37: Hero, Suffer Heroically 187

Entry 38: Hero, Do Something About Suffering..............................193

Entry 39: Hero, Porn Will Destroy You and Those You Love 197

Entry 40: Hero, Dance to the Rhythm of God's Grace 203

Entry 41: Hero, Get Ready for Battle...209

Entry 42: Hero, Finish the Race 215

Epilogue: Hero, May I Pray For You?...219

Notes 222

A SPECIAL NOTE

My wife and best friend, Vicki, will make this journey with us. Throughout the book, she adds her insight and perspective. I know that you will be inspired, just as I have always been, by her courage, wisdom, and deep love for the Great Hero. As the depth of her comments engage you, the words of Benjamin Disraeli come to life, "Nurture your mind with great thoughts; to believe in the heroic makes heroes." I'm a better man because of her...she compels me to live heroically.

My wife's name originates from "Victoria," which is derived from the word "victory." Victory means winner or conqueror; in other words: hero. Her name fits her perfectly. The statement "Behind every good man is a woman" is wrong. Standing beside every good man is a hero.

Vicki is my hero.

I will steady him with my hand;
with my powerful arm I will make him strong.
Psalm 89:21 NLT

INTRODUCTION

YOU EXIST TO BE A HERO | Whether it was childhood battles with toy soldiers, dreams of making the game-winning shot, or visions of winning an epic battle like William Wallace in the movie *Braveheart*, there has been a time when you sensed the mysterious, heart-pounding call to be the hero you were created to be.

It's probably been awhile since you have felt anything like that power. The call to be a hero has been drowned out by the soul-defying sounds of demanding emails, pressing phone calls, hounding debt, and the accumulation of ordinary, everyday disappointments in life. Perhaps your "fairy-tale ending" turned into something less than perfect so you have settled for being less than you were created to be. But even now, deep down, you know that you were destined for something else, something momentous, something that matters.

Your soul is tattooed with the desire to be a hero. It's what you were created for. So why aren't you living like a hero?

WHERE HAVE ALL THE HEROES GONE? | There could be many reasons why you are not living a heroic life. Exhaustion, emptiness, shattered dreams, and loneliness are just a few of the hero-killers that come between a man and the life he is meant to live.

Many men are exhausted. In our fast-paced, multitasking, twenty-first-century way of surviving, words like stressed, drained, and maxed-out describe many men. The average man is drowning in a turbulent sea of obligations, unmet expectations, and duties that even Superman would struggle to fulfill. Maybe it is even making you angry.

Think about it: You are asked to work longer and harder at your job while at the same time you need to make sure you are spending time with your wife and kids. You feel required to provide enough so that you can own a nice home for your wife, your kids can wear the "right" labeled clothes, and you can fully fund your family's future. And if you are a Christ-follower, pile on your need to have a ministry, tell your friends about Jesus, and attend a weekly accountability group with other tired men. After a long day at work, it's no wonder men sink into a zombie-like state in front of the TV, drink a six-pack, and flip channels aimlessly for hours until they stumble into bed.

This book is about living with an energized passion.

Many men have a deep ache in their soul that reminds them every morning that they are empty and unfulfilled. Do you ever find yourself saying something like this: "I've got a good job. I love my wife. I adore my kids. If all this is true, then why am I so frustrated and unsatisfied?" If you are single, it may sound like this: "I have no purpose! I don't know what to do with my life; my job sucks. If it wasn't for the money, I would fire myself and do something I really love…if I only knew what I would love to do!"

I can relate. Despite playing six years in the NFL, an insistent and gnawing cry echoed in my soul as I surveyed the landscape of my life in the summer of 1997: "There's got to be more to life than this." Man, I was the walking embodiment of the "American dream." Through football, I escaped the West Side ghetto of San Antonio, Texas, only to find myself in another one. This ghetto, however, had all the right external pleasures one could possess: a smokin'-hot wife, a sweet Lexus sedan with shiny rims, a brand-new home, great vacations, fame, an elite professional occupation, financial stability, and extra money to provide for my grandparents, mother, and siblings. The outer decorations of my life looked good, but my internal reality looked like a gruesome car wreck. The external "stuff" I possessed could not fill the Grand-Canyon-sized hole in my soul. Can you relate to that hole-in-your-soul feeling?

We are empty and unfulfilled because we've been using the wrong map, which has taken us to the wrong destination.

This book is about using a new map that will guide you to a new destination, producing a new heroic you.

The dreams of men have been shattered by the cold reality of life. Things haven't quite worked out the way you've planned, have they? Who grows up dreaming, "My first marriage will end in a burning flame of anger, adultery, and insecurity"? Who thinks, "I can't wait to have a job that I hate so much that I want to vomit when I get to the office"? Who lifts the bottle up saying, "I want my alcoholism to destroy my life and family the way Hurricane Katrina destroyed New Orleans"?

This book is about learning to pick up the shattered pieces and dreaming big again.

Many men are lonely. Perhaps you're saying, "Derwin, I have friends—lots of them." Do you really? I'm not talking about the superficial relationships you have that revolve around Fantasy Football, *Guitar Hero*, *24*, and your job. I'm talking about real friends or, as we used to say where I grew up, "homeboys." The kind of homeboys that will help you construct yourself into a man of honor, sacrifice, integrity, fierce love, and wisdom—not false friends that will help you deconstruct your life. This book is about true friendships and leaving a legacy that impacts a generation of men for years to come.

It's about learning to live a heroic life—and fighting for the life you were created to live.

SHADOW MAN | Did you ever chase your shadow when you were young? Shadows look like real people, but they are not. Have you noticed how the majority of sitcoms usually cast men as shadows? Let me explain. In many sitcoms, the husband is presented as a joke. He's portrayed like Al Bundy, the unheroic father in *Married with Children*. He's dumb, passive, hopelessly self-centered, un-inspiring, lacking the respect of his children, and he is, of course, more in love with his favorite NFL team than his wife. "Shadow man" does not inspire us to be men of risk-taking courage, fierce love, and life-giving sacrifice like the great abolitionist Frederick Douglass, *Braveheart*'s William Wallace, or my high school football coach, D. W. Rutledge. "Shadow man" is as shallow as a one-inch-deep puddle of muddy water.

But here's a thought, and this thought may hurt: Think of it as an immunization shot—painful, but for our own good. Could it be that "shadow man" is who we have become? In our tiredness, our emptiness, our loneliness, have we become shadows of the men we were created to be?

Men, as you read these words, I pray that a searing-hot anger is rising in you. As I write these words, I'm even getting ticked! Will you join me in an act of revolutionary rebellion against "shadow man"? Will you join me in a declaration of war against anything that is enslaving us and keeping us from living a heroic life? It is time for an all-out insurgency.

WHAT YOU NEED TO KNOW | Before we go any further, this reality must be burned into your soul: You, my friend, were created to be a hero. You have been forged by the divine Craftsman to be a great warrior of honor, sacrifice, integrity, fierce love, and wisdom. With His very own hands of grace and power, and with unhindered love and patience, God has created you to be a hero.

I want you to do a little exercise with me. Grab your PDA or some paper off your desk and write yourself a message of encouragement. Mine would say, "Derwin, you have been created to be a great warrior of honor, sacrifice, integrity, fierce love, and wisdom. You've been created to be a hero." Read the message again…slowly and prayerfully. Marinate in it. Let the truth of this message soak deep down into your soul.

Here's the deal. You and I will always live according to how we see ourselves. Do you see yourself as a hero? The mirror of our lives is not what we say—it is what we do. What does your mirror say to the world?

I can confidently say that you were created to be a hero because you were made in the image of the Great Hero—God. Do you believe that, friend? My son, Jeremiah, looks like me and acts like me—why? Because he is made in my image. My DNA brought him into being and is forever present in him. Well, the Great Hero brought you into being, and His divine DNA is in you. Theologians call this reality the Imago Dei (image of God). God created you to be so intimate with Him that you reflect Him. This book is about getting to know the Great Hero so well that His greatness rubs off on you and is present in your life.

WHO IS THIS BOOK FOR? | Maybe you are a man in the third quarter of his life, and the reality that the game clock is running out is challenging you with this question: "What difference have I made in this world?"

Perhaps you are a single twenty-something guy and the questions that haunted me when I was your age are stalking you, too: "What is a man?" "How do I treat a woman?" "How do I deal with disappointment and failure?" "Can someone teach me about sex?" "How do I focus my life and find a meaningful career that I love?"

Maybe you're a young husband with small children and a beautiful wife, and you've come to realize that no matter how hard you try you can't love her the way she deserves. Maybe you work way too much chasing the "American dream" and your children are being neglected by you, too.

Possibly you're a young mother with two boys you deeply love. Not a night goes by that you do not look into their eyes and pray, "God, how can I raise them to be men that live a life of honor, dignity, and significance?"

No matter your stage in life or your gender, this book is for you or someone you know and love.

I want to do great things; I want to live a life that matters. As a woman, I also want to be a hero. I want to be able to help my husband, my son, and my daughter be all they were created to be and live lives of significance and fulfillment.

V. Gray

WHAT'S THIS BOOK ABOUT? | This book is about journeying to your destiny; it's about becoming the hero that God has uniquely crafted you to be. For us to get to our destination, we need a divine GPS to guide us. The first part of this book is entitled "The Upward Journey." In it, we will reflect and meditate on the characteristics of the Great Hero in whose image we are created. This part of the book is the most essential; it is impossible for you and I to be who we are created to be if we do not know our God and Father intimately.

The middle part of the book is called "The Inward Journey." This section will set our eyes on how God's Good News forges a new identity in the heart of a man. This new heroic identity will free you from your past failures, and empower you to live a heroic life in the present, so you can live a life that positively impacts the future.

The final part of the book is called "The Outward Journey." Everything you do in life happens as a result of what's going on in your heart. When I say "heart," I do not mean the muscle that pumps blood; I mean the core of who you are that determines what you do. In this section, we will learn how the hero that you are meant to be is empowered by the Great Hero Himself to live a life of God-style love, maximum impact, and soul-gripping adventure.

HOW TO USE THIS BOOK | This book is designed to be read on your own or with others in a group. Going on a journey is always better when traveling with friends, although sometimes we do need to walk alone. You may be a mature man helping to develop a younger man into a hero or a group of women desiring to walk with your sons and husbands in shaping them to be heroic men or a posse of brothers seeking to sharpen one another like iron sharpens iron. Whatever your situation, you will find this book a great traveling companion.

There will be forty-two entries in this book. At the end of every daily entry, you will find the "Head, Heart, Hands" application section. Head will focus on the "big thought" of the day; Heart will focus on what you are feeling as a result of reading the daily entry; and Hands will focus on what to do with what you've learned.

ARE YOU READY? | Today is the day that "shadow man" dies and the hero is born.

On Mission with the Great Hero,

Derwin Gray

SECTION ONE

THE UPWARD JOURNEY

ONE

THE GREAT HERO
IS THE GREAT CREATOR

And God saw everything he had made, and, behold, it was very good.
GENESIS 1:31 KJV

THE DREAM | I grew up in the ghetto on the west side of San Antonio, Texas, near the Lincoln Courts housing projects. The scope of my world was about three square miles of small, weather-beaten homes and old schools that were way past their primes. The way I traveled the world beyond my streets was through watching TV shows like *Wild Kingdom* and *Hawaii Five-O*, the 1980 versions of *Animal Planet* and *CSI: Miami*.

When you're poor and living on government assistance, vacations and family trips around the country to see our nation's diverse landscape aren't a consideration for you or your friends. Since our families couldn't take us to the exotic places we saw on TV, we decided to take ourselves. Two of my best friends and my older cousin decided that we were going to Hawaii.

We wanted to run on Waikiki Beach.

We wanted to taste the Pacific saltwater.

And I think, most of all, we wanted to buy an original Hawaiian shirt.

We were determined to save money, board an airplane, and fly to Hawaii. We were inspired to experience the beauty we saw once a week through our TV sets with the huge "rabbit ear" antennas. Nothing was going to stop us... except the reality that we were all poor. I think I ended up saving something like $21 dollars and some change. My friends and cousin didn't do any better.

Of our crew that saved money to go to Hawaii, I'm the only one who ran on Waikiki Beach. I'm the only one who tasted the Pacific saltwater and bought an original Hawaiian shirt. The reason why I went and they didn't was because I earned a football scholarship to Brigham Young University.

Let's pause for a moment. Many of you are thinking, "How did a non-Mormon African-American end up at Brigham Young University, a school dedicated to the Church of Jesus Christ of Latter-Day Saints, also known as the Mormon church?" Strap on your seat belt…you are in for a wild ride.

I grew up sitting on the lap of my grandmother, learning bits and pieces of Jehovah's Witness doctrine. (Are you confused yet?) So even though our family never prayed together or practiced any kind of religious activity that I can remember, I was sort of a Jehovah's Witness who accepted a football scholarship to a Mormon university and who, in reality, worshiped the false god called football!

A god is someone or something that gives you your identity and mission in life. Football did that for me.

So how did I become a Christ-follower? It was through the influence of the Naked Preacher! I told you, strap on your seatbelts! During my rookie year with the Indianapolis Colts (1993), I noticed a linebacker on the team that was rather unique. After practice he would take a shower, dry off, and wrap a towel around his waist. Then he would pick up his Bible and begin walking like a 1970s pimp as he approached guys in the locker room, asking them this strange question: "Do you know Jesus?" It seemed exceedingly odd to me to see a half-naked black man walking around with a Bible in a NFL locker room. Besides, I was in the NFL to build my empire and fulfill my dreams (which eventually led to misery).

Out of curiosity and a dose of fear, I asked the veterans on the team, "What's up with the half-naked black man walking around and saying 'Do you know Jesus'?" They said, "Don't pay any attention to him; that's the Naked Preacher."

As I look back at my first encounter with the "Naked Preacher," I see that it was ingenious of him to ask the question, "Do you know Jesus?" Why? Because in the Bible it says, "Now this is eternal life, that they may know you, the only true God, and Jesus Christ, whom you have sent" (John 17:3 NIV).

The word "know" in the Greek language means to experience. Basically, the Naked Preacher was asking the most important question that can be asked: "Are you experiencing a life-defining love relationship with the living God of the universe?"

After practice one day in 1993, the Naked Preacher said to me, "Rookie D. Gray, do you know Jesus?" That question changed my life. Over the next five years, Steve Grant, aka "The Naked Preacher," and a few other teammates who followed Jesus, journeyed with me through success, injuries, and failure. On August 2, 1997, alone in a small dorm room at training camp in Anderson, Indiana, I embraced Jesus as my God, my Savior, and my life.

Okay. Back to the story.

At BYU, I played against the University of Hawaii in Honolulu three times in four years. In fact, I chose BYU over other schools because I knew I would get a chance to go to Hawaii.

IT'S BETTER IN PERSON | Hawaii was better in person. What I saw on TV could not compare to the Pacific breeze that said "good morning." Over the years I've gotten to see some beautiful places: As a freshman football player, I stood speechless before the awe-inspiring Wasatch Mountains in Provo, Utah, that overshadowed our practice field; I've flirted with my wife as we relaxed in the turquoise-colored waters of the Dominican Republic; I've danced with my daughter, Presley, on the white-sand beaches of the Cayman Islands.

If you slow down and pay attention, you will realize that the Great Hero is displaying His greatness through the beauty that constantly surrounds you. Creation is waiting to be discovered, appreciated, and enjoyed.

OUR SMALLNESS—HIS HUGENESS | Since my days of growing up in San Antonio, I have experienced some beautiful places. In all my travels, the most beautiful place in the world to me has become Victor, Montana. My wife was born and raised in western Montana, so once a year we go stay with her family in Victor. It's like the movies—her parents have a beautiful log cabin, a river teaming with trout, and a backyard full of deer with an occasional moose stopping by to hang out.

At night, I love to go outside with my father-in-law and simply look up. Because there are no city lights, the heavenly lights are on display. Being from the city and currently living in the city, I see why Montana is called Big Sky Country—there are so many stars.

When I think of the universe and its size, I realize my smallness and the Great Hero's hugeness. Astronomers estimate that there are 300 billion stars in our galaxy, the Milky Way. Additionally, there are 300 billion galaxies in our universe, and each star is estimated to be 30 trillion miles apart. When the Space Shuttle travels in outer space, it travels at an incredible speed of over 17,000 miles per hour. Our universe is so vast that it would take the Space Shuttle over 201,000 years to travel from one star to another![1] No wonder a hero named King David said, "When I look at your heavens, the work of your fingers, the moon and the stars, which you have set in place, what is man that you are mindful of him, and the son of man that you care for him?" (Psalm 8:3–4 ESV).

David looked into heavens, saw the creative power of the Great Hero, and was humbled by God's awesomeness and his own smallness. It's hard to imagine a universe so big that the number of all the stars in it is about equal to the number of grains of sand on every beach in the world. And you know what? The Great Hero knows them all by name! Listen to another hero named Isaiah, who reflects on this reality:

> Lift your eyes and look to the heavens: Who created all these? He who brings out the starry host one by one, and calls them each by name. Because of his great power and mighty strength, not one of them is missing" (Isaiah 40:26 NIV).

HIS IMAGE IS TATTOOED IN YOUR SOUL | The Great Hero who created the universe set the stars in place and knows them by name! He did this by His "great power and mighty strength." Reflect on the great things God has created. Whatever your mind came up with, it doesn't compare to *you*. This means you are of incalculable worth, capable of doing things you never thought possible, because the image of the Great Hero is tattooed on your soul.

Do I really believe that I am God's greatest creation?
Do I believe it when I look at my husband, my child,
my neighbor, or even my "enemy"? Do I view myself
and others as that valuable?

V. Gray

God's greatest and most fantastic creation looks at you in the mirror every morning, buys Starbucks coffee with you, and, yes, even cuts you off in morning traffic. If you do not embrace this fact, you will never become the hero you were created to be. Listen with your heart to these verses of sacred writing:

"So God created human beings in His image" (Genesis 1:27 NCV).

"Oh yes, you shaped me first inside, then out; you formed me in my mother's womb. I thank you, High God—you're breathtaking! Body and soul, I am marvelously made! I worship in adoration—what a creation! You know me inside and out, you know every bone in my body; You know exactly how I was made, bit by bit, how I was sculpted from nothing into something" (Psalm 139:13–15 THE MESSAGE).

Never, ever forget: Your life was not an accident. You are not an irrelevant nobody. According to God, you are His image-bearer!

BECOMING THE HERO YOU WERE CREATED TO BE | What you admire above anyone or anything else is what you *worship*. Whatever or whoever you worship, you *will* become like. And whoever you become like will determine how you live. The first step in your journey toward living a heroic life is for you to admire the Great Hero, the One whose image you bear.

HEAD

- Tonight, slowly and prayerfully, read Psalm 8:3–4 and Isaiah 40:26. After reading these passages, go outside and simply spend some time looking into the sky. Marinate in the thought of God's hugeness and your smallness.
- Reread Genesis 1:27 and Psalm 139:13–15 and *affirm* that you are made in the image of God. Affirm that you and all of humanity is God's greatest creation.

HEART

- What feelings are being triggered in your heart as you read today's entry? Do you feel humbled by these thoughts? Do you feel empowered as God's greatest creation? Write down your feelings and ask God to help you work through them. Friends, this is going to take some work. Be patient and be honest with God and yourself. It will be worth it!

HANDS

- Since you are tattooed in the Great Hero's image, you, too, are a creator. Think of ways to use your creative ability to bless other people at your job, at school, in your family, and in your neighborhood.

THE GREAT HERO
IS OUR GREAT FATHER

Father of the fatherless...
PSALM 68:5 ESV

MEN AND THEIR FATHERS | I've spent a lot of time being angry at my father. Anger sat in my soul like acid, eating away at me for years. My last memory of him being involved in my life in a positive way was when he bought me a yellow bike for my sixth birthday; however, one of my more vivid memories of him is from when I was in eighth grade. I played basketball and, surprisingly, he showed up for one of my games. He yelled from the stands. I'm not sure what he was yelling, but it was impossible for me to focus on the game after that because I kept saying to myself, "Why are you here, Dad?"…"I haven't seen you in years!"…"Don't you dare sit next to my mom!"

That night I played my worst game of the year. Then, to make matters worse, he walked into the locker room and talked to my basketball coach after the game. It was clear that my father had a substance abuse problem. The coach and I made eye contact but quickly looked away from each other, pretending not to know what was going on. A deep, gaping father-wound was slashed in my heart. That moment was a turning point in my life. I decided to live as though he did not exist. I became determined to show my dad that I could make it without him.

Many men fail to live a heroic life because they are being held prisoner by their father-wounds.

"RUN, LOUIE, RUN!" | In Texas, football is a religion! The stands were filled to overflowing for our Friday night battles under the lights. I saw lots of faces in the crowd, but I never saw the face of my father. I played two years in middle school, four years in high school, four years in college, and six years in the NFL, but my father has never seen me play football in person. I would have loved to hear his voice from the stands yelling, "Son, I am proud of you!"

I remember this one kid named Louie on my high school football team whose dad *was* at every game and even at just about every practice. At the end of practice, we would run a conditioning drill called "sprint laps," which involved running in a pattern across the field. As we ended the sprint laps in the end zone, one voice rose above all the other voices: "Run, Louie. Run, Louie…go, son!" Louie's dad constantly cheered for him.

Some of my teammates and I made fun of Louie because of his dad. Now that I look back with thirty-eight-year-old eyes, I see that I laughed at Louie because I longed for my own dad to be there cheering for me.

Many of you may be workaholics who neglect your families because you falsely think that if you work harder and longer, you will hear your dad say, "Son, I am proud of you." Also, many of you struggle with encouraging your sons or daughters because your father never encouraged you.

Many of you men fail to live heroic lives because you are captive to the father-wounds left long ago. Anger and unforgiveness rule in your heart instead of love. These feelings toward your father are like *you* drinking poison and hoping *he* dies.

———

Even as adults, we will always be someone's child. I wonder how often we hold our parents to an impossible standard of perfection, one that only our heavenly Father can meet. Lord, open my heart to accept, forgive, bless, honor, and cherish my parents.

V. Gray

———

YOUR FATHER IS NOT PERFECT AND NEITHER ARE YOU | As I look back at the memory of my dad attending that basketball game, I suspect he thought he was encouraging me with his yelling. And in light of his struggles with alcoholism, it was a miracle that he even showed up at all.

Here's the deal: *None* of our fathers are perfect, and none of us will be perfect fathers. But there is a Perfect Father who loves you and cheers you on. His love and encouragement toward you is not based on your goodness, but on His. Never forget that through faith in Jesus, you have unlimited and unhindered access to *the greatest father of all*, God. Let these words marinate in your soul:

> What marvelous love the Father has extended to us! Just look at it—we're called children of God! That's who we really are (1 John 3:1 THE MESSAGE).

> But to all who believed him and accepted him, he gave the right to become children of God. They are reborn—not with a physical birth resulting from human passion or plan, but a birth that comes from God (John 1:12 NLT).

What issues from my own experiences am I hurling at my husband as the father of our children? What unrealistic expectations am I asking him to fulfill as a dad?

V. Gray

EMBRACING THE GREAT HERO AS YOUR GREAT FATHER | Every little boy naturally sees his father as a godlike figure, and I was no different. Since I was raised in a non-Christian home, my view of God was colored by my earthly father. In my mind, God was out there somewhere, but he was not near. It was not until I embraced God as my Father that I was *empowered* to forgive my earthly father and develop a healthy relationship with him. I also realize that my dad did the best he could considering the life-crippling addictions that prevented him from being the hero he was created to be. Some of you are so angry at your fathers that it is ripping your guts out. Maybe you can still feel the heartbreak from when your dad abandoned you and your mom for his secretary. Maybe the bruise that his fist left on your face has gone away, but the bruise in your heart remains unhealed. Maybe you still feel inadequate around your dad because he is never satisfied with anything you ever do.

Men, living in the pain of the past ends today! You have a Hero for a Father that will never let you down! Right now, through the Great Hero, your Great Father, choose by His power to march in love and forgiveness toward the heroic life that awaits you.

HEAD

- Read Psalm 68:5, Matthew 6:9, and 1 John 3:1.
- Ask God to cement in your heart the reality that He is your Father and that He loves and accepts you.

HEART

- What feelings are being stirred in you as you read today's entry? Are you living with anger toward your father? If so, how is this anger keeping you from being a hero? Record your feelings in your journal and ask God to help you work through them.

HANDS

- Write your father (or your mother) a letter, even if they are dead. Tell him that you forgive him, and that you love him. If you do not feel this way, pray and ask God to give you the power that is needed.
- If you have a son or daughter, write them a letter. Tell them that through God's empowerment you are going to be the father that they need. List specific ways that you want to be a hero to them. Let them know that you *will not* be perfect but that you promise to always lead them to the Father, who is perfect.
- Using three three-by-five-inch index cards, write out Psalm 68:5 on one of the cards. Then do the same for Matthew 6:9 and 1 John 3:1. Place these note cards where you can see and reflect on them daily.

THREE

THE GREAT HERO WANTS TO KNOW YOU FACE-TO-FACE

In the beginning was the Word, and the Word was with God, and the Word was God.
JOHN 1:1 ESV

BIG BULL | I love my son, Jeremiah. When he was a baby, we would look into each other's eyes as I held him in my right hand. The weight of knowing that one day he would want to be like me forced me to my knees in prayer. My prayer went something like this: "God, please help me to be like You because one day he's going to want to be like me."

Jeremiah is now nine years old. His nickname is Big Bull. We call him that because he's four-feet-nine, weighs 86 pounds, and wears men's size seven-and-a-half shoes! Jeremiah does a lot of things well. He excels in school, is especially kind to younger children, and is an amazing athlete. I have had the privilege of coaching the eight- and nine-year-olds on his football team, and at times he'd do things that would blow my mind.... I'd look to my assistant coach and say, "Did he just do what I thought he did?"

Despite all the things he knows and all the things he does well, they are not as important to me as this: I want my son to know that his papa loves him for who he is, not for catching touchdowns or acing tests. I want an *intimate* relationship with my son—for my son to love and know me and for me to love and know him.

FACE-TO-FACE | Jeremiah has taught me a lot about intimate relationships. When he was about three years old, if he was talking to me and my face was not pointed toward his, he would grab my face and turn it so it was. He wanted my full attention. He wanted me to be face-to-face or "intimate" with him; it's as if he was saying, "Dad, I want you to be so close to me that *you see into me*."

Let's take a moment to pull back the curtains of eternity. John 1:1 communicates it this way, "In the beginning was the Word, and the Word was with God, and the Word was God." This passage teaches us that the Father and the Word, who is Jesus, have always existed. There was never a time that they did not exist in relationship to each other. Another insight into the mystery of this passage is the English word "with." This word in Greek is *pros*, which expresses the idea of being face-to-face. "Face-to-face" in the Hebrew mind-set expresses an intimate love relationship. God the Father and God the Son are eternally "face-to-face."

Wrap your heart and mind around this: From all eternity, the Great Hero has existed in perfect relationship within Himself. Our heavenly Hero is a *tri-personal being*. He is the Father, the Son, and the Holy Spirit (Hebrews 9:14). Before the moon, the stars, oxygen—even before time— God was and is. The Father, the Son, and the Holy Spirit have been eternally "face-to-face."

God created you to be face-to-face with Him. This is what Jesus means in John 17:3 when He says, "And this is real and eternal life: That they know you, the one and only true God, and Jesus Christ, whom you have sent" (THE MESSAGE). Until you are face-to-face with Him, it will be impossible to be *truly* face-to-face with anyone else.

———

Knowing that God already knows what's in my heart,
I can be free to be face-to-face with Him—because He
loves me anyway! This frees me up to be more
face-to-face with those I love.

———

V. Gray

Many men fail to live a heroic life because they do not know how to live face-to-face with God, themselves, and others. In the midst of an argument with your wife, does she say, "Why don't you talk to me?" Friend, you crawl into the cave of silence because you do not know how to be face-to-face with her.

Do you have a hard time with conflict resolution at work because you stuff your feelings? You do this because you do not know how to live face-to-face. Young men, do you have a hard time talking to women about how you feel about them? You get the idea.

The Great Hero is calling your name and inviting you to know Him face-to-face and live face-to-face with others.

HEAD

- Prayerfully read John 17:3 and Philippians 3:7–10. God created you to know Him face-to-face.
- The most important relationship you will ever have is with the Great Hero. All your other relationships will flow from this one relationship. Pause and reflect on this truth.

HEART

- What are you feeling as you read today's entry? What do you think about God wanting to know you face-to-face? Are you uncomfortable with God wanting to know you at this level? How do you think your relationship or lack of a relationship with God has impacted your relationships with others? Write down your feelings and ask God to help you work through them.

HANDS

- Get alone. Take a walk and talk to God about wanting to know Him face-to-face.
- Practice looking people in the eyes when they talk to you. Do not multitask.

THE GREAT HERO
IS OUR GREAT PROTECTOR

Because he holds fast to me in love, I will deliver him;
I will protect him, because he knows my name.

PSALM 91:14 ESV

CONFESSION TIME AND A FAST FORTY | I've got a confession. When I was in elementary school, I was bullied by three different boys. Yes, a former NFL team captain was bullied. If one of them wanted my money, he got it. If one of them wanted the coat I was wearing that day, he got it. You name it, if they wanted it, I gave it to them with no resistance.

When the bell at the end of the school day rang, I sprinted to get home. It was like the TV show *Animal Planet*. I was the impala...they were the lions. If I could just outrun them to my house, I was safe...at least for that day. I'm often asked, "How did you get so fast?" I got fast because I had a lot of practice running from the boys that bullied me.

CONFIDENCE | When I was running full-tilt toward home, something interesting happened the closer I got to my house. The feelings of fear decreased, and feelings of confidence increased. This change in attitude occurred because the closer I got to my house, the closer I was to my protector. I had an older cousin named Squeaky. Do not let the cute name fool you—Squeaky had a reputation in the neighborhood. Simply put, he was known for beating people down. Nobody messed with Squeaky unless they had a desire to get a black eye. My confidence grew the closer I got home because my confidence was not in my fighting skills, but in his. Squeaky protected me. He was family.

ARE YOU TIRED OF BEING BULLIED? | Are you tired of being bullied by your own selfish desires that keep you from living a life of significance? Are you tired of your life being destroyed by the bully named pornography and sexual addiction? Are you tired of being bullied by self-sabotage because you see yourself as a failure instead of a hero? If you are, it's time that you run home to your hero and protector. God, the Great Hero, is your Great Protector!

Many men fail to live a heroic life because they have given in to a bully or are trying to fight life's bullies in their own strength instead of in God's strength. Stop trying to fight your bully in own your power; let God fight for you. Think about it—the Great Hero and Protector is the ruling and reigning cosmic ultimate fighting champion.

THE THREE-HEADED BULLY | Men (and women), we have three bullies that want to destroy us. The first is the *world* (1 John 2:15). We are entrenched in a culture that consists of interlocking structures and systems that influence our life. The jobs we hold, the society we live in, and the government we live under influence our lives. The world becomes one of our bullies if we are not allowing the Great Hero to shape our lives. For example, many men live in outrageous debt because the world dupes them into thinking that if they own the biggest house and most expensive car, they've realized the American dream. Soon they awaken from this dream only to find themselves under a mountain of debt that is now a nightmare.

The second bully is the *flesh* (1 John 2:16–17). When I use the biblical word *flesh*, I do not mean your skin or muscles. The Bible teaches that we humans have a strong desire within us to do what we know is not right. Even the apostle Paul struggled in this fight. You can hear the anguish in his voice through these verses:

> For I do not understand my own actions. For I do not do what I want, but I do the very thing I hate…. For I do not do the good I want, but the evil I do not want is what I keep on doing (Romans 7:15, 19 ESV).

Think of it this way: When was the last time a child had to be taught to be selfish? By nature they are selfish. We must teach children to share. And God must teach us to love and do what is right.

Maybe your flesh rises up when you are on a business trip away from your wife. You sit tired and bored in a lonely hotel room. You pick up the remote and begin to aimlessly flip channels. You soon realize that you can buy a pornographic movie with the click of a button. You say to yourself, "No one will know." That's the flesh in action.

The third bully is the *devil*. There is an evil being with great power named Satan. He is filled with hatred for God and you. His sick and twisted aspiration is to keep you from being the hero God has created you to be. He has a gang of demons that roam the earth like lions seeking to destroy you (1 Peter 5:8).

Lord, help me to not be critical of the men in my life. Instead, I want to pray for them to overcome their "bullies" by relying on You.

V. Gray

LEARNING TO FIGHT IN HIS POWER | Once in fifth grade, I was at the gym with my cousin, boxing. Unexpectedly, one of the boys that bullied me showed up. He started putting on gloves to box me, and I found myself getting ready to fight this guy that had terrorized me for years. Before I knew it, we were in the ring. When we started fighting, I was in a crazed frenzy, backing him into a corner and beating him down! At the end of the round, he was balled up in the fetal position. I thought to myself, "I am crushing him. All these years I've been afraid of this." From that moment on, I was not bullied anymore. My cousin, my protector, had taught me to fight. *His strength and presence gave me the confidence to win.*

Are you ready to go from being bullied to beating down your bullies? If so, run home to your Protector, whose presence and strength will empower you to defeat the bullies in your life.

HEAD

- God is your Protector. Through His presence and strength He will empower and teach you how to defeat the world, the flesh, and the devil.

- Slowly read Colossians 1:13–14; 2:13–15; and Ephesians 6:10–20 and see how you can defeat the three-headed monster.

- Because Jesus is victorious over the three-headed bully, through faith in Him, His power now belongs to you. See Romans 6:5–6.

HEART

- What are you feeling in your heart as you read today's entry? How has the *world*, the *flesh*, and the *devil* caused havoc in your life? Be specific. Write down your feelings and ask God to help you work through them.

HANDS

- Take your specific list of the ways the world, the flesh, and the devil have caused havoc in your life. Then read and pray that Psalm 91:14, Romans 6:11–13, and Romans 8:37 would be realized in your life.

- Take that list and share it with a friend or mentor. Ask them to pray that these passages will be realized in your life.

FIVE

THE GREAT HERO
IS THE GOD OF INTEGRITY

Holy, holy, holy, is the LORD almighty; the whole earth is full of his glory.
ISAIAH 6:3 NIV

NEEDED: MEN OF INTEGRITY | Our nation is in desperate need of heroes.

Bernard L. Madoff is a former NASDAQ Stock Market chairman and founder of his own securities firm where thousands of people and even charities trusted him with their entire savings. He was arrested and charged with fraud in what federal prosecutors called a Ponzi scheme that could involve losses of more than $60 billion.

Kenneth Lay, former CEO of Enron, was convicted of a fraud that destroyed his company and cost 20,000 employees their jobs. Many of them also lost their entire life's savings, and investors were swindled out of millions. Before he served a day in prison, he died while on vacation in Colorado.

New York Governor Eliot Spitzer, who gained national celebrity for persistently pursuing Wall Street corruption, was caught on a federal wiretap arranging to meet with a high-priced prostitute at a Washington hotel. Mr. Spitzer resigned in shame with his wife holding his hand.

Do I reach out to those who are without the love of Christ when I see their lack of integrity? Do I pray for them, or do I throw stones?

V. Gray

According to a large-scale survey by the Josephson Institute of Ethics, 30 percent of high school students within the last year have stolen from a store and 64 percent have cheated on a test. The research also showed that 92 percent of the students said they were satisfied with their personal ethics and character and 74 percent affirmed that "when it comes to doing what is right, I am better than most people I know."[1]

Our nation is in desperate need of heroes who embody integrity.

WHAT IS INTEGRITY? | The biblical understanding of integrity "points to a consistency between what is inside and what is outside, between belief and behavior, between our words and our ways, our attitudes and our actions, our values and our practices."[2] The Bible has another word for integrity— *holiness.* God *is* integrity. He is holy, and through participating in His offer of life, we, too, can be empowered to become men and women of integrity (2 Peter 1:3–4).

CLOSE ENCOUNTER OF THE LIFE-CHANGING KIND | Isaiah was a prophet during the reign of King Uzziah. His job was to proclaim to the nation of Israel that God's judgment was coming because of their lack of integrity. Israel, during this time, was a moral wreck. Instead of displaying God's integrity to the world, they brought shame to His Name and destruction to their lives.

Isaiah encounters the God of integrity and is humbled (Isaiah 6:1–8). Isaiah saw the Great Hero and began to *unravel* because he was overwhelmed with God's holiness, with His integrity. Face-to-face with absolute perfection and majesty, Isaiah says, "Woe is me!… I am ruined" (Isaiah 6:5). In essence, he is saying, "I am falling apart at the sight of the God who *is* integrity. And now I realize my lack of integrity and my sin."

Isaiah is also hopeful in God's presence. The Great Hero, out of His limitless love and *justice*, must eradicate sin the same way a good doctor must eradicate a limb with gangrene. If a limb with gangrene is not cut off, it will eventually kill the entire body. In the same way, the God of integrity can only be in a relationship with a person of *equal* integrity. When Isaiah encounters God, an angel takes away Isaiah's guilt and wipes away, or atones, for his sin

(Isaiah 6:6–7). This is a beautiful picture of what Jesus does for humanity by His life, death, and resurrection. Because of our lack of moral perfection, we cannot be in a relationship with the God of moral perfection. So God, out of unrestrained love, sent Jesus to remove our guilt and wipe away our sins by dying on the cross in our place (1 John 4:9–10).

Just like the next person, I am incapable of being a person of integrity without the perfection of Christ.

V. Gray

Can you imagine the hope Isaiah must have experienced to know that God had removed all his guilt and then covered over all his sins? Friends, it is my prayer that you, too, have experienced the removal of all your guilt and the covering over of all your sin through Jesus. Encountering the God who is integrity changed Isaiah forever! No wonder he responded the way he did:

> Then I heard the voice of the Lord saying, "Whom shall I send? And who will go for us?" And I said, "Here am I. Send me!" (Isaiah 6:8 NIV).

God's integrity provokes Isaiah to "live on mission." The Great Hero removes your guilt and covers your sin so that you can share in His integrity. When a person embraces Jesus as his God, Savior, and Friend, they also receive His integrity or holiness as a free gift (1 Corinthians 1:30; Hebrews 2:11). The cry of the Great Hero's heart is for you to be a person that reflects His integrity. Eugene Peterson describes a man of integrity this way:

> But what happens when we live God's way? He brings gifts into our lives, much the same way that fruit appears in an orchard— things like affection for others, exuberance about life, serenity. We develop a willingness to stick with things, a sense of compassion in the heart, and a conviction that a basic holiness permeates things and people. We find ourselves involved in loyal commitments, not needing to force our way in life, able to marshal and direct our energies wisely (Galatians 5:22–23 THE MESSAGE).

Because God gave Isaiah His integrity as a gift, Isaiah boldly and unwaveringly calls Israel back to living a heroic life of integrity as a nation. Can you imagine how wonderful a place the world would be if all of us lived lives of integrity? Let's not just imagine it—let's be men of integrity like Isaiah and live on mission so others can be changed by the God of integrity also.

HEAD

- ❧ God is the God of integrity (holiness) and has created you to reflect His integrity to the world. Read Isaiah 6:1–8.
- ❧ God has given you His integrity as a free gift so you can live a life of integrity. Read Hebrews 2:11, 1 Corinthians 1:30, 1 Peter 1:15, and review Galatians 5:22–23.
- ❧ Read John 12:41. Who did Isaiah see?

HEART

- ❧ What feelings are being stirred in you as you read today's entry? In the past, how have you felt about God being holy? Has today's entry changed your view of God's holiness? Be specific. Record your feelings and ask God to help you work through them.

HANDS

- ❧ Write down the ways you have not lived with integrity. Ask the Holy Spirit to empower you to live a life of integrity.
- ❧ Share what you wrote down with men that you trust—maybe a mentor or your accountability group so they can pray for you.

SIX

THE GREAT HERO
IS IN CONTROL

And now do not be distressed or angry with yourselves because
you sold me here, for God sent me before you to preserve life.

GENESIS 45:5 ESV

SHATTERED DREAMS | Most of us think God exists to fulfill our dreams.

We pray to get that new job,

to win the game,

to impress a girl.

Many of us pray for a comfortable life where we are in control. In reality, we exist to fulfill God's dream of reconciling the world unto Himself (2 Corinthians 5:19; Colossians 1:19–20). God is so committed to fulfilling His dream that, if necessary, He will allow our little self-centered dreams to sink like the Titanic. My dream of playing in the NFL for ten years sank to the bottom of the sea of disappointment at the 50-yard line in Texas Stadium, home of the Dallas Cowboys.

My last play in the NFL was not that much different than any other play. I sprinted downfield on kickoff coverage. I collided with a blocker. I turned to the right; he turned to the left. But in the midst of this turning, my left foot got stuck in the Astroturf. When that happened I heard the medial collateral ligament in my left knee snap, and on the outside of that same knee, I heard the bone crack. I had been hurt before. This time, however, I knew my career was over.

As I was on my back writhing in pain, I looked up through the hole in the roof of Texas Stadium. Like an angry five-year-old, I told God, "Don't you know I have a dream of playing for ten years?" On the very field where I grew up wanting to compete, my dream was shattered into a million pieces.

In the midst of my pain, God was leading me to a new and better dream—His dream.

The Great Hero is in control of His entire creation. This means our tri-personal God is before all things, beyond all things, has created all things, upholds all things, knows all things, can do all things, and controls all things. What a profound mystery. God is in control of His creation, yet He unfolds His plans through our actions. Wow! The more I journey with Jesus, the more I realize that when I allow for mystery in the faith, the more I understand. And the more I try to take mystery out of the faith, the less I understand.

Do I realize that God's dream for my life is much bigger than my own? Have I released control over what I think "should be" and trusted the Great Hero with my life... and my husband's and kids' lives, too?

V. Gray

To help us learn to embrace how God is in control of His universe, even in the midst of our broken dreams, let's look at the story of Joseph.

THE DREAMER | Joseph was the favorite son of Jacob—and his ten older brothers knew it. They hated him, especially after their father gave Joseph a "robe of many colors" (Genesis 37:3–4), a gift signifying that he would inherit more than his brothers.

Joseph was also a dreamer. God used dreams to show Joseph that one day his brothers would bow down to him. Young Joseph didn't keep this secret from his brothers. They finally had enough of Joseph's boasting and their father's favoritism toward him. They stripped him of his robe and threw him into a pit, telling their father he was dead. Later they sold him to traders who took him to Egypt and enslaved him to Potiphar, an Egyptian officer of the Pharaoh's guard (see Genesis 39).

Can you imagine the hurt and disappointment Joseph must have experienced? His very own brothers had done this evil to him. And where is God in the midst of this betrayal? Glad you asked. Listen with your heart:

The LORD was with Joseph, and he became a successful man, and he was in the house of his Egyptian master. His master saw that the LORD was with him and that the LORD caused all that he did to succeed in his hands. So Joseph *found* favor in his sight and attended him, and he made him overseer of his house *and* put him in charge of all that he had (Genesis 39:2–4 ESV).

Friends, what catapults you toward heroic living is the ability to trust God and embrace His steadfast love even when our dreams are shattered.

Joseph continued to find disappointment in His life—like being falsely accused of rape by Potiphar's wife and thrown into prison. But even in the midst of that trial, God never left him.

But the LORD was with Joseph and showed him steadfast love and gave him favor in the sight of the keeper of the prison.... And whatever he did, the LORD made it succeed (Genesis 39:21, 23 ESV).

While in prison, Joseph begins to interpret dreams. Through using this God-given gift, he finds himself second-in-command in all of Egypt (Genesis 41:39–45). A terrible famine, which Joseph knew would come, hits Palestine—where his brothers lived. His father, Jacob, sends all his older sons to Egypt to purchase grain from Joseph. The teenage boy they threw into the pit and sold is now a strong man and unrecognizable to them. But Joseph recognizes them and remembers his dreams from years before (Genesis 42:8–9). Joseph wept loudly as he told his brothers who he was (Genesis 45:2).

And he said, "I am your brother, Joseph, whom you sold into Egypt. And now do not be distressed or angry with yourselves because you sold me here, for God sent me before you to preserve life.... So it was not you who sent me here, but God (Genesis 45:4–5, 8 ESV).

God, who is in complete control, allows Joseph, through the evil actions of his brothers, to save many lives and ultimately preserve the Hebrew nation so Jesus could be born through it and save the world.

Joseph knew something about the Great Hero that you need to know if you are going to live a heroic life: God is in control of His universe. He is sovereign.

PICKING UP THE PIECES | My original dream died in Texas Stadium, but a new, larger heroic dream from God was born. After my career-ending injury, God catapulted me into sharing His message across America and has graciously turned me into a pastor and author. Over the years, I have received thousands of emails and letters from people whose lives have been impacted by God through the ministry He has given me. The cheers in the stadiums of my former dream pale in comparison.

Friends, you have been created to live a heroic life. In the midst of your shattered dreams, trust our sovereign God. He will use your life to impact the lives of others. Remember, *our disappointments are His appointments.*

HEAD

- What catapults you toward living a heroic life is the ability to trust God even when your dreams are shattered because He is sovereign and He loves you with an unrelenting, limitless love.
- Read 2 Corinthians 5:19. You exist to fulfill God's dream. What might this look like in your own life?

HEART

- What are you feeling as you read today's entry? Over the years, how has God allowed your dreams to be shattered? Are you ready to live His dream? Write down your feelings. Ask God to empower you to live His dream.

HANDS

- Revisit Genesis 39:2–4, 21–23. Ask God to empower you to be like Joseph in the midst of adverse circumstances.
- Pray these passages of scripture into your life, your son's life, and the lives of the men you influence.

SEVEN

THE GREAT HERO IS FAITHFUL

He who calls you is faithful; he will surely do it.
1 THESSALONIANS 5:24 ESV

THEOLOGY AND LEARNING TO RIDE A BIKE | My daughter Presley has a scar on her left elbow. She has that scar because I failed her.

When Presley was about four, we went outside for the big day—the day she would learn to ride her bike without training wheels. As I began to coach her, she refused to keep pedaling when I let her go.

I said, "Honey, you have to keep pedaling, or you are going to fall."

"Papa, I'm afraid to keep pedaling because I am going to fall," she said.

"Baby, I will not let you fall.... I will be there to catch you. Trust me."

Of course you know what happened next. She fell and gashed her left elbow. As a young father, I was crushed. Here I was telling my firstborn child, "I will not let you fall," and then I did. Her elbow was bleeding, she was crying, and her mother was on her way outside to see what was going on. After things settled down, with tears in my eyes, I said, "Presley, we learned a great lesson today. Your papa is unfaithful to keep all his promises to you, but God is not. He is always faithful to keep His promises to you. That's why we worship Him and not me." Presley's scar is a continual remainder to us to trust God, because He and He alone is faithful to keep His promises.

GOD of the Angel Armies, who is like you, powerful and faithful from every angle? (Psalms 89:8 THE MESSAGE).

WHAT IS THE FAITHFULNESS OF GOD? | Unlike humanity, the Great Hero is faithful because He is all-powerful, all-knowing, unchanging in His character, always truthful, unconditionally loving, and in control over His creation. In a world of unfaithfulness, it is great to know that our life rests on God, the eternal rock of faithfulness.

He is faithful to provide and ensure the eternal kind of life. God loves the world with such an intense passion that He gave the greatest gift heaven had to offer—His Son. Whoever embraces Jesus will freely receive eternal life. This *eternal kind of life* is not just a "get-out-of-hell-free" pass. Eternal life means that the very God of heaven and earth now lives in you (Galatians 2:20). Eternal life is not just a place where you go when you die. It is a life you possess today, and it extends into the vast reaches of eternity. In an act of immeasurable mercy and grace, through Jesus, the Great Hero shares His life with you. Slowly and prayerfully reflect on this sacred truth:

> God, who got you started in this spiritual adventure, shares with us the life of his Son and our Master Jesus. He will never give up on you. Never forget that (1 Corinthians 1:9 THE MESSAGE).

He is faithful to provide love so that we can love. Life is about loving people; it's about relationships. The quality of your life is a direct result of how you relate to and love others. God wants your relationships to be healthy. The Good News is that God gives you Himself so you can love people with His kind of love. This "God kind of love" is deposited in you through faith in Jesus:

> Love is patient and kind; love does not envy or boast; it is not arrogant or rude. It does not insist on its own way; it is not irritable or resentful; it does not rejoice at wrongdoing, but rejoices with the truth. Love bears all things, believes all things, hopes all things, endures all things. Love never ends (1 Corinthians 13:4–8 ESV).

Can you imagine having relationships where God's kind of faithful love is expressed through you as you submit your will to His? Friends, you do not have to imagine it—you can experience it because God is faithful to provide the love you need.

Is submitting your will to His will easy? No. Many of you have been wounded deeply by people who have not been faithful, and if you haven't already, you will. But through the life and power of our God of faithfulness, we can be energized to love people…even when we don't want to.

As I meditate on the great grace that God has given me when I have not been perfect, I can choose to release those I love from the standards of perfection I have for them, trusting that God will lead each of us to become more like Him.

V. Gray

He is faithful to provide resources to overcome sin. The heart of God is broken when you choose to live with unforgiveness, uncontrollable anger, addictions, racism, jealously, self-centeredness, and cutthroat competition. It destroys you and damages your relationships. God is faithful to provide you with an eternal kind of life in which His all powerful Spirit empowers you to live a life of "love, joy, peace, patience, kindness, goodness, faithfulness, gentleness, and self-control" (Galatians 5:22–23). Your job is to submit your will to His and ask Him to release His life through you.

He is Faithful to provide resources to meet your physical needs. God has graciously given you the skills to be the best that you can be. Hear me carefully: *You cannot be anything you want to be, but you can be all that God has created you to be.* He wants you to develop and enhance your abilities, because that brings Him honor and it brings you purpose and joy. Your skills are also God's gracious gift to you so that you can have your physical needs met, as well. A hero lives *in* and *for* God. Reflect on this passage:

> People who don't know God and the way he works fuss over these things, but you know both God and how he works. Steep your life in God-reality, God-initiative, God-provisions. Don't worry about missing out. You'll find all your everyday human concerns will be met. Give your entire attention to what God is doing right now, and don't get worked up about what may or may not happen tomorrow. God

will help you deal with whatever hard things come up when the time comes (Matthew 6:32–34 THE MESSAGE).

He is Faithful to provide for your eternity. God is not only faithful to take care of your *today*, He is also faithful to take care of your *eternity*. The life, death, and resurrection of Jesus Christ is an unstoppable force, and all those who trust in Him will live eternally as He does (1 John 3:2). Unlike the unfaithfulness I exhibited to my daughter, Presley, the Great Hero is faithful in keeping His promises. Rest in this sacred truth:

> Let not your hearts be troubled. Believe in God; believe also in me. In my Father's house are many rooms. If it were not so, would I have told you that I go to prepare a place for you? And if I go and prepare a place for you, I will come again and will take you to myself, that where I am you may be also (John 14:1–3 ESV).

BECAUSE HE'S FAITHFUL YOU CAN BE FAITHFUL | The more you are "face-to-face" with the Great Hero, the more His faithfulness will be woven into your life. Friends, you can live a heroic life because He is faithful.

HEAD

- ❧ Reread 1 Thessalonians 5:24, Psalm 89:8, and Matthew 6:32–34. God is faithful to keep His promises.
- ❧ Reread 1 Corinthians 1:9, 1 Corinthians 13:4–8, Galatians 5:22–23, and John 14:1–3. God is faithful to provide you with all you need for life.

HEART

- ❧ What are you feeling as you read today's entry? What does it mean to be faithful? How do you feel God has or has not been faithful to you? Be specific. Write down your feelings and ask God to help you work through them.

HANDS

- ❧ Choose someone close to you and write a letter in your own words about God's faithfulness and how He is committed to being faithful to them.

THE GREAT HERO HAS ALWAYS BEEN THE GREAT HERO

From everlasting to everlasting you are God.

PSALM 90:2 ESV

HOW WOULD YOU LIVE DIFFERENTLY? | How would you live differently if you knew you were going die within a few years? In the winter of 2005, I went to my doctor for a routine physical. No big deal, right? The doctor took some blood for testing. The results came back a few weeks later—and I needed to see a liver specialist because I had Hepatitis C. Hepatitis C is a blood-borne disease caused by a deadly virus that attacks the liver. It has no cure. It will kill you. But how could I contract a disease that is contracted through blood transfusions and IV drug use? I had never had a blood transfusion, and I wasn't an IV drug user. Yet my blood work showed I had this life-ending disease.

To make matters worse, I received this terrible news while I was speaking in Florida at a youth camp in the middle of nowhere. That night the only thing I could do was curl up with my Bible. I could not sleep. During my sleepless night, I asked myself some tough questions like, "Are you making the most out of the life God has given you?"

After seeing the liver specialist, he confirmed that I did not have Hepatitis C, but my life was forever changed. I had a new appreciation for life, for people, and for what I was on the earth to do.

TO BE MOST LIKE GOD | We are most like the Great Hero when we live in the *precious present*. God has always been. He is the One who was and is and always will be. He has no father or mother. The Great Hero has no past or future. He has no yesterdays or tomorrows; He lives in the eternal now. Being a hero means that we learn to live in the now or the *precious present* because it is all we really have. And it is in this moment where we live and reflect God.

COMPETING PERSPECTIVES | An *earthly* perspective leads to an unheroic life. This perspective demands that you neither trust nor depend on God because it is based on what is seen. In contrast, the *eternal* perspective produces a heroic life because it is deeply rooted in the unseen; therefore, it requires you to radically depend on God. Meditate on the chart below.[1] Ask yourself which life characterizes yours:

UNHEROIC	HEROIC
Pleasure	Knowing and loving Jesus
Recognition of People	Resting in Jesus' approval
Popularity	Servanthood
Wealth and Status	Integrity and Character
Power	Humility
⬇	⬇
Emptiness	Fulfillment
Delusion	Reality

Living with an earthly perspective dehumanizes you. It strips you of being the hero you were created to be. And when you are not the hero you were created to be, your life and the lives of those you influence will be negatively affected.

Many men shipwreck their lives and those they influence when they live as though the *earthly* is *eternal*. They devalue people and treat them as a means to an end. They see their jobs as a way to buy stuff and to pay off their debt caused by buying too much stuff, rather than using their God-given abilities to glorify Him. The unheroic man spends his life chasing the next thing, never alive to the precious present.

*Am I so busy in pursuing temporary things that
I don't have time for people? Do I know how to rest in
God's approval so that nothing distracts me from
pursuing and serving Him?*

V. Gray

LIVING IN THE PRECIOUS PRESENT | When a man sets his mind on seeking and loving the eternal God of the eternal kingdom, he is awakened from mediocrity and becomes alive to the present moment, where life is lived. The *precious present* is where you choose to place the needs of others above your own. The present is where you choose to become vulnerable to your wife. The present is where you choose to value people, not because of what they can do for you, simply because they are valuable to God. As you embrace living in the now, instead of taking people and life's circumstances for granted, you will see their sacredness (Ephesians 5:15–16).

*Lord, help me to enjoy the present moment so that I may
communicate to my family the depth of love and value
I place on each one of them.*

V. Gray

Are you living an unheroic life by squandering it through living with an earthly perspective? Friends, the Great Hero, out of love and wisdom, has set eternity in your hearts (Ecclesiastes 3:11). Do not surrender your divine birthright! Fight to be the hero you've been created to be.

LIVE LIKE YOU ARE DYING | Men, I thought I was dying. And you know what? I am. And so are you. Don't waste another precious present.

HEAD

❧ Reread Psalms 90:2. The Great Hero has always been and always will be God. Because He is eternal, He lives in the precious present. And because you are made in His image, you are most like God and fully alive when you live in the precious present.

HEART

❧ What feelings are stirring in you as you read today's entry? When you contemplate the chart that shows the competing perspectives, which perspective most reflects your life?

❧ How has this impacted your life? Write down your feelings and ask God to empower you to work through them.

HANDS

❧ This weekend, take a half day and find a place to be alone.

❧ During this time, pray and ask the Holy Spirit to empower your life to reflect God by living in the precious present.

❧ Apologize to God and the people you have neglected because you've been living with an earthly perspective.

NINE

THE GREAT HERO IS GREAT IN WISDOM

My son, be attentive to my wisdom; incline your ear to my understanding.
PROVERBS 5:1 ESV

DECISIONS THAT IMPACT GENERATIONS | You are going to make decisions that will not only impact your life but the lives of future generations. Think about that. The decisions you make today will impact someone's tomorrow. In light of this massive responsibility and privilege, it is crucial that you become a wise man.

Wise men make wise decisions that bless people.

Unwise men make unwise decisions that curse people.

Which type of man do you want to be?

WISDOM: WHAT IS IT? | Wisdom is the skill to live life well. And learning to live in God's wisdom is a process called discipleship. A disciple is a student who learns from a teacher. *The Teacher* is Jesus, the Great Hero who is the embodiment of wisdom (Luke 2:52). His goal for you is to imitate His wise life through the power of the Holy Spirit. In living a wise life, you become a *blesser* of people, just like He is.

A disciple is not above his teacher, but everyone when he is *fully* trained will be like his teacher (Luke 6:40 ESV).

If you want to be a wise man, you need to go to the Great Hero, who is the source of all wisdom. Sit at His feet and learn from Him.

WHAT IS GOD'S WISDOM? | God's wisdom is His ability to orchestrate and choose the best means in which to accomplish the best end results. Because God is all-knowing, He has the knowledge to make wise choices. Because He is all-loving, we know that His choices are in our best interest. And because He is all-powerful, He has the power to achieve His end results by the means He chooses. In the governing of His universe, God makes no mistakes. He is the Papa who truly knows best.

Do I look to God and His wisdom when I face crucial decisions, or do I trust in my own "wisdom," which is limited, at best? Lord, help me to model to my spouse and children the need to seek Your wisdom in all of life.

V. Gray

"DAD, I DO NOT NEED YOUR WISDOM" | When my son Jeremiah was five years old, he went through a stage of not taking advice from me when I tried to coach him in football. My son acted like he knew more about football than me. I would patiently say, "Son, your father was nominated for the Pro Bowl; I was a team captain in the NFL, and in college...I was pretty good. I have some wisdom and knowledge that will help you, if you will listen."

Think about how foolish it was for my son not to take my advice, considering my expertise in football. Hero-in-the-making, it is fifty-seven-billion times more foolish for you to not take the Great Hero's advice when He is trying to teach you how to live. God desires that you receive His wisdom so you can live a "blessed life" that becomes a blessing to others (Proverbs 3:13).

NO GOD LIKE THE GREAT HERO | The Great Hero's wisdom and knowledge is perfect (Job 36:4), mighty (Daniel 2:20), unlimited (Psalm 147:5), unsearchable (Isaiah 40:28), wonderful and beyond human comprehension (Psalm 139:6). No one compares to the Great Hero (Isaiah 44:7)! The Great Hero is wise, and out of a desire to see you live a heroic life, He freely offers you His wisdom so He can influence every decision you make (Proverbs 2:6–7).

HOW DO YOU GET WISDOM? | The way to gain full, unhindered access to God's wisdom is by *respecting* Him. Proverbs 9:10 says it this way: "Wisdom begins with respect for the Lord, and understanding begins with knowing the Holy One" (NCV). We are led back to a "face-to-face" encounter with God. The more we *know* and *experience* Him in the everydayness of life, the more we *become* like Him in the everydayness of life. This is God's goal for us.

He desires for His wisdom to guide every decision you make. Drink deeply from His fountain of wisdom; it never runs dry. God's wisdom is found in the Bible, through praying and meditating on His truth, and in living in community with wise men who can walk alongside you as you make decisions.

WISDOM TO UNDERSTAND THE GIFT | We live in a time where men who claim to follow the Great Hero know more about their favorite sports team or their job than they do about the eternal kind of life Jesus gives to them as a gift. The Great Hero is "so rich in kindness and grace that he purchased our freedom with the blood of his Son and forgave our sins. He has showered his kindness on us, along with all wisdom and understanding" (Ephesians 1:7–8 NLT).

If you want wisdom and insight into how great this eternal kind of life is, just ask God. He wants you to be "filled with the knowledge of his will in all spiritual wisdom and understanding, so as to walk in a manner worthy of the Lord, fully pleasing to him, bearing fruit in every good work and increasing in the knowledge of God" (Colossians 1:9–10 ESV).

WISDOM FROM ABOVE IMPACTS YOUR LIFE DOWN BELOW | The Great Hero's wisdom teaches you how to have successful relationships. Slowly take in James 3:13–18:

> Who is wise and understanding among you? By his good conduct let him show his works *in* the meekness of wisdom. But if you have bitter *jealousy* and selfish ambition in your hearts, do not boast and be false to the truth. This is not the wisdom that comes down from above, but is earthly, unspiritual, *demonic*. For where jealousy and selfish ambition exist, there will be disorder and every vile practice. But the wisdom from above is first pure, then *peaceable*, gentle, open to reason, *full*

of mercy and good fruits, *impartial* and sincere. And a harvest of righteousness *is* sown in peace by those who make peace (ESV).

ONE LAST THOUGHT AND REASSURANCE | The Great Hero is so committed to seeing you develop into a wise person that He will give you wisdom, if you ask Him:

> But if any of you needs wisdom, you should ask God for it. He is generous and enjoys giving to all people, so he will give you wisdom (James 1:5 NCV).

With a God like this in your corner, you can't help but become a hero.

HEAD

- Reread Job 36:4, Daniel 2:20, Psalm 147:5, Isaiah 40:28, and Psalm 139:6. You can trust God's wisdom to guide your life.
- God's wisdom is His ability to orchestrate and choose the best means in which to accomplish the best end results.
- God desires that you live a wise life. Read James 1:5 and Proverbs 2:6–7.

HEART

- What are you feeling as you read today's entry? How have the decisions you've made without God's wisdom impacted your life and those around you? How about the decisions you've made using God's wisdom? Write down your thoughts. This can be both painful and healing. Ask God to empower you to be honest with yourself.
- Read James 3:13–18. Does your life reflect wisdom from above?

HANDS

- Before you make any major decisions, ask God for His wisdom by praying James 1:5 and Proverbs 2:6–7.

TEN

THE GREAT HERO IS LOVE

Because God is Love...
1 JOHN 4:8 ESV

CREATED TO ENJOY BEING LOVED | The Great Hero is love. And you have been created to enjoy being loved by Him. Your life has no greater goal...no higher priority than to know the love of God. That's why Paul, a recipient of God's love, wrote this to you:

> I once thought these things were valuable, but now I consider them worthless because of what Christ has done. Yes, everything else is worthless when compared with the infinite value of knowing Christ Jesus my Lord. For his sake I have discarded everything else, counting it all as garbage (Philippians 3:7–8 NLT).

To know God is to be loved by God, and to be loved by God is to know Him. You were created "from love, of love, and for love."[1] Your life will be fragmented, broken, and disjointed without God's love to make you whole.

In a world where nothing is free, it may shock you to realize that God's love truly is free. You do not have to pay for it by being good or by achieving some moral standard of acceptability (Ephesians 2:8–9). The Great Hero's love for you has nothing to do with your behavior. Neither your faithfulness nor your unfaithfulness changes in the slightest degree God's love for you.

> He has not punished us as our sins should be punished; he has not repaid us for the evil we have done. As high as the sky is above the

earth, so great is his love for those who respect him. He has taken our sins away from us as far as the east is from west. The LORD has mercy on those who respect him, as a father has mercy on his children (Psalm 103:10-13 NCV).

The Great Hero cannot love you any more than He already does. His love for you is infinite! That means it is limitless. His divine love is so great toward you that it cannot be measured—just received and enjoyed. Meditate on the words of this poem as they express the vastness of God's love:

> Could we with ink the ocean fill
> And were the skies
> of parchment made,
> Were every stalk on earth a quill
> And every man a scribe by trade,
> To write the love of God above
> Would drain the ocean dry,
> Nor could the scroll
> contain the whole
> Though stretched from sky to sky.[2]

FINDING REST IN HIS LOVE | If you do not park your soul in His refuge of love, you will spend your entire life looking for love in all the wrong people, places, and possessions. Hero-in-the-making, despite the darkness of your past, your soul-crippling habits, or the painful memories that haunt you, you are created to be loved because you bear the image of the God who is love.

Men, I'm not talking about some weak, sentimental love. I'm talking about God's fierce, life-empowering love. I'm talking about God's holy love that will shake the foundations of your being. I'm talking about the kind of love that will turn you into a hero, like Jesus. Listen and receive into your heart the truth of God's love for you:

> I pray that from his glorious, unlimited resources he will empower you with inner strength through his Spirit. Then Christ will make his home in your hearts as you trust in him. Your roots will grow down into God's love and keep you strong. And may you have the power

to understand, as all God's people should, how wide, how long, how high, and how deep his love is. May you experience the love of Christ, though it is too great to understand fully. Then you will be made complete with all the fullness of life and power that comes from God (Ephesians 3:16–19 NLT).

A heroic life is a life of power because it is rooted deeply in the love of Jesus. Are you tired of living a powerless life? If you are, right now in holy silence, ask the Great Hero to give you power to understand how wide, how long, how high, and how deep His love is.

HOW DO YOU KNOW GOD LOVES YOU? | He's freely given you air to breathe, food to eat, and skills to make a living. He's given you a family, imperfect as they are. He's given you friends. Your life explodes with God's love toward you. But the ultimate act of His immeasurable love for you is the gift of His Son, Jesus:

> This is how God showed his love for us: God sent his only Son into the world so we might live through him. This is the kind of love we are talking about—not that we once upon a time loved God, but that he loved us and sent his Son as a sacrifice to clear away our sins and the damage they've done to our relationship with God (1 John 4:9–10 THE MESSAGE).

The response to such an extravagant gift is simple yet profoundly difficult. We are to love Him back (1 John 4:19), but in order to do that, we must surrender our pride at the feet of His throne of grace (Matthew 5:3). God loves you, so you can enjoy and love Him back. And as you enjoy being loved by God, supernaturally you will begin to enjoy the freedom that loving your neighbor brings to your life (1 John 4:11).

THE FREEDOM LOVE GIVES | Are you living a fear-driven, self-centered, performance-based life? If you are, you know from firsthand experience the unbearable, crushing weight this adds to your life. Are you ready to unload it? Do you want to turn it around? Think about the freedom you will have when you stop being mad at your father or mother…or when you stop holding anger against your spouse or your coworker. Think about the freedom you will have when you stop hating the person that molested you. Imagine the freedom you will have when you *start* loving yourself. When I say loving yourself, this simply means seeing yourself as God sees you. Through participating in Jesus' life by faith in Him (Romans 6:4–6), you are a loved child of God. Never forget, God's "grace humbles us without degrading us and elevates us without inflating us." [3]

Friends, a hero is a man clothed in the uniform of love.

> So, chosen by God for this new life of love, dress in the wardrobe God picked out for you: compassion, kindness, humility, quiet strength, discipline. Be even-tempered, content with second place, quick to forgive an offense. Forgive as quickly and completely as the Master forgave you. And regardless of what else you put on, wear love. It's your basic, all-purpose garment. Never be without it (Colossians 3:12–15 THE MESSAGE).

Do I "dress in the wardrobe God picked out for me"? Lord, if I am to live a life that reflects You, I need You to do this in and through me each day so that I am who I need to be for those in my sphere of influence.

V. Gray

Friends, this uniform of love is not something that you have to work to acquire. It is a gift that God gives you to wear and live out in your relationships (Ephesians 4:22–23).

THEY WILL KNOW BECAUSE YOU LOVE | By loving your neighbor, who is anyone God graciously places in your path, the people in your everyday life will know you are a disciple of Jesus. Did you catch that? Hero-in-the-making, you live *in* and *for* the reputation of God (Matthew 5:16). When you embrace God's love, you are magnifying His reputation among people that have not met Him "face-to-face."

A new commandment I give to you, that you love one another: just as I have loved you, you also are to love one another. By this all people will know that you are my disciples, if you have love for one another (John 13:34–35 ESV).

The Great Hero's love for you compels Him to desire your eternal joy, which is a life where you enjoy being loved by Him, loving yourself, and loving others (Mark 12:29–31). And because He controls His universe and is all-powerful, He will see that this happens in your life as you *participate* with Him by submitting your will to His. With a Papa like this, you are ensured of being a hero! Fulfill your destiny!

HEAD

- ❧ Reflectively and slowly, reread 1 John 4:8, Philippians 3:7–8, Ephesians 3:16–19, 1 John 4:9–11, and John 13:34–35.
- ❧ The words "God is love" mean that love is an essential attribute of God. It expresses the way the Great Hero is by nature.
- ❧ God desires and *empowers* you to enjoy being loved by Him and to enjoy loving yourself and others. Read John 15:9.

HEART

- ❧ What feelings are stirring in your heart as you read today's entry? How have your views of God been challenged?
- ❧ Before reading this entry, did you think God loved you? More importantly, are you experiencing God's love?
- ❧ How do you feel now that you know that God loves you the way He does? Be specific. Write down your feelings and ask God to help you work through them.

HANDS

- ❧ Colossians 3:12–15 describes the uniform of a hero. Read it and write it on a note card. Place this note card where you can see it daily.
- ❧ Read Ephesians 3:16–19. Memorize it.
- ❧ And never forget: It is the Great Hero's power that energizes you to live a heroic life!

ELEVEN

THE GREAT HERO IS THE GREAT "I AM"

God said to Moses, "I AM WHO I AM."

EXODUS 3:14 ESV

LIVING LIKE A HERO | The Great Hero is inviting you to live a heroic life. This means that God will ask you to do courageous things that are way beyond what you think you are capable of. He will launch you into turbulent, chaotic, seemingly no-win situations.

One of the reasons many men fail to live a heroic life is because they are afraid to do things that are beyond their natural ability. They are afraid to give up the familiar and the comfortable for the unfamiliar and uncomfortable. They are afraid to trust God in supplying His supernatural resources to the task He is calling them to execute. But if you truly want to live heroically, get ready, because God will invite you to do things that often seem undoable.

To ensure that you get the job done, the Great Hero whispers in your ear, "*I AM* with you," and "*I AM* whatever you need." Let's take a look at a God who says His name is *I AM* and a hero named Moses.

I AM WHO I AM | *I AM* is the sacred name of God. It is so sacred that observant Jews to this very day will not write it or even say it. The name *I AM* expresses that God is the *self-existent, eternal, mighty One*. But it means more than that, too. This name speaks of our tri-personal God's faithfulness and unwavering commitment to love and be with His people in all of life's circumstances. God says, *I AM* "is my name forever, and thus I am to be remembered throughout all generations" (Exodus 3:15 ESV).

The God of the Bible does not ask us to do things that He does not join us in doing and empowering us to do. "He who calls you is faithful; he will surely do it" (1 Thessalonians 5:24 ESV).

MOSES AND THE BIG STORY | By the time Moses was born, Israel was a nation in captivity. Slaves in Egypt, the Israelites had fallen low from the days when Joseph was the trusted advisor to Pharaoh. A new pharaoh in a new age only saw the rising threat Israel posed to his power. He ordered the slaughter of Hebrew sons (Exodus 1:16), among them, the baby Moses.

Moses survived by the courage and quick thinking of his mother and ultimately grew up in Pharaoh's own household as an adopted son of a princess. Despite this lavish lifestyle, Moses saw the suffering of his people. One day, out of anger, he killed an Egyptian taskmaster who was beating a Hebrew slave. Moses was found out, and he had to run for his life.

FORTY YEARS OF PREPARATION | Little did he know that for the next forty years of life, Moses would be preparing for a task that was beyond his natural ability. Then one day he encountered the Great I AM in a burning bush. God had a huge, seemingly impossible mission for Moses—"I will send you to Pharaoh that you may bring my people, the children of Israel, out of Egypt" (Exodus 3:10 ESV).

Push the PAUSE button for a moment. Before Moses could go on this mission, he needed forty years in the desert to prepare His character. Moses had no clue that the forty years in the desert was God shaping his character for this future mission. Like Moses, you may be in a desert season of life…and God, too, is shaping your character for your future rescue mission.

Perhaps you think God has forgotten you.

Perhaps you think His voice is silent.

One truth that has been anchored in my soul is that God does His best work in us during our desert seasons of life, and I've come to realize that He is speaking the loudest when I can't hear Him.

HOLY TERROR AND FREEDOM | At the burning bush, when Moses realized that he was in the presence of God, he hid his face in sheer terror of God's awesome presence. Then God, who was filled with compassion for His people Israel, told Moses that He had seen their sufferings:

> "I have come down to deliver them out of the hand of the Egyptians and to bring them up out of that land to a good and broad land, a land flowing with milk and honey" (Exodus 3:8 ESV).

> God then says, "I will send you to Pharaoh that you may bring my people, the children of Israel, out of Egypt" (Exodus 3:10 ESV).

God called Moses to live as a hero. And for you to live as a hero means that God will call you to do things you cannot possibly do in your own power.

Can you imagine what Moses was thinking? "God, you want me to go to Pharaoh...the most powerful man on the planet...and tell him to let his workforce go so they can worship You?... And, by the way, in case you have forgotten, Pharaoh wants to kill me."

God always desires the best for His people. And the best for His people is for them to be free so they can serve Him. In serving Him, they experience true freedom to live. Are you scratching your head? Let me explain.

In Exodus 3:12, God wants His people to *serve* Him. In the Hebrew language, the word *serve* means "slave." God, in essence, is saying, "My people will be free to worship me and reflect my goodness to each other and the world when they are my slaves." *It is in slavery to God that you experience true freedom.* And true freedom is a life of God-style love (1 Corinthians 13:4–8; Mark 12:29–31).

MOSES' EXCUSES AND GOD'S PROVISION | Moses gave God excuses for why he couldn't do what God asked him to do. First he asked God, "Who am I that I should go to Pharaoh and bring the children of Israel out of Egypt?" (Exodus 3:11). *He doubts he's the right man for the job.* Do you ever feel like Moses, like God has the wrong man?

God reassures Moses that he is the right man for the job and that He is with Moses. Hero-in-the-making, God is with you, too! When my son was a little guy, he would have bad dreams at night that would cause him to call out my name. From a deep sleep, I could hear the fear in my son's voice. In a matter of moments I was at my son's bed, whispering in his ear, "Papa's here. I am with you, son."

Your Papa does not sleep. He hears the fear in your voice, and He is whispering in your ear, "Papa's here. I AM with you, son."

In the midst of your wife leaving you, I AM with you.

When the job you held down for twenty years becomes outsourced, I AM with you.

In the midst of your loneliness as a single, I AM with you.

In the midst of your wife dying of cancer, I AM with you.

It is amazing to ponder the reality that whatever my struggle, God says, "I AM." I want to live in the truth that the Great Hero is the great I AM to my every need and desire. This is living by faith.

V. Gray

The Great I AM is the Great Immanuel—God is with you at all times, in all places, and in all circumstances (Matthew 1:23). The wise words of a hero named Saint Patrick, who God sent on a seemingly impossible mission to take His message to the nation of Ireland, reinforces this truth:

> Christ be with me, Christ within me,
> Christ behind me, Christ before me,
> Christ beside me, Christ to win me;
> Christ to comfort and restore me;
> Christ beneath me, Christ above me,
> Christ in quiet, Christ in danger,
> Christ in hearts of all that love me,
> Christ in mouth of friend and stranger.

HE'S WHATEVER YOU NEED | Not only is the Great Hero with you, *He is whatever you need* to get the job done. God informs Moses that His Name is I AM WHO I AM. He is the God of Abraham, Isaac, and Jacob (Exodus 3:14–15). The Great I AM is unlimited in His power, in control of His universe, matchless in His wisdom, eternally compassionate, and enormous in love. With an awesome God like this, you cannot help but be a hero!

ONE MORE EXCUSE | Moses gives one more excuse. He tells God he has a speech problem. I can relate to this excuse because I grew up with a compulsive stuttering problem. In 1999, when God called me to travel and preach, I argued with Him. I told Him that I was a stutterer and that if He wanted me to speak He would have to do it. Not too long after that, He corrected my speech problem.

God is with you and God is whatever you need to get the job done. He is the Great I AM.

SET THE CAPTIVES FREE | God is calling you to be a Moses to someone enslaved to sin. Maybe your son is enslaved to drugs. Maybe your best friend is having an affair. Maybe your marriage is chained down by unforgiveness.

Just like in Moses' day, some people will choose the familiar life-suffocating surroundings of slavery rather than being free (Exodus 16:3). Do all that you can do to snatch them from this trap (Jude 1:24). Whoever God is calling you to set free, never forget, the Great Hero is the Great I AM. This means He is with you and He is whatever you need.

HEAD

- ✤ Read Exodus 3:2–14, John 8:58, and Matthew 1:23.
- ✤ What does the name I AM mean?
- ✤ Never forget that the Great I AM is with you and will be whatever you need to complete the mission He has given you.

HEART

- ✤ What feelings are being triggered as you read today's entry? How does it feel knowing that God is with you and will be whatever you need to complete the mission in which He is calling you?

- Are you in the desert right now? How does it change your perspective to know that God is shaping your character during this time?
- What are your excuses to God for not doing what He has called you to do? Be specific. Write down your feelings and ask God to empower you to work through them.

HANDS

- Has God placed someone in your life who needs to be set free from sin?
- Write down their names and pray for them. Share these names with your accountability group or a mentor and have them pray with you. Begin to look for opportunities to impact their lives.

SECTION TWO

THE INWARD JOURNEY

HERO, WHERE ARE YOU?

God called to the Man: "Where are you?"
GENESIS 3:9 THE MESSAGE

CREATING AN ILLUSION | Have we become masters at being who we are not? As if we were master builders, we try to construct our lives based on the false illusion of who we want others to think we truly are. We fool no one but ourselves. Those who know us well know who the person in the mirror really is. We fear that if God, our wife, our mom, our dad, or our friends knew the *real* us, they would run from us because of the dark areas in our lives.

Why wouldn't we hide our true selves? We are simply running down the same path placed before us by Adam, the biological father of the human race. He taught us everything we know about running and hiding from God when we blow it.

You may be right—all may run—except for One. And the One who would not run away from you would actually run toward you…and not with a closed fist of condemnation but with open arms of grace and restoration.

IN THE GARDEN | The Great Hero created Adam and Eve "from love, by love, and for love" so that they could love. He created our first parents to know Him and to represent His greatness to all of creation. But Satan, the crafty enemy of God and man, deceived Adam and Eve. He persuaded our parents to doubt God's goodness: "For God knows that when you eat of it your eyes will be opened, and you will be like God, knowing good and evil" (Genesis 3:5 ESV). It was not wrong for Adam and Eve to want to be like God. They were His image-bearers. He created them for that very reason—to be like Him. Adam and Eve could never share God's attributes of being all-powerful, all-knowing, self-existent, or sovereign. Theologians call these God's *non-communicable* attributes. However, like you and me, Adam and Eve were created to share in God's *communicable* attributes like love, joy, peace, patience, kindness, goodness, faithfulness, gentleness, and self-control (Galatians 5:22–23). These attributes describe what humanity's original design was. Imagine a world of humans living heroically like this. That would be heaven on earth.

Adam and Eve wanted to be like God *without* God empowering them to do so. Their revolt was refusing to live in *dependency* on God. In essence, sin is telling God, "I can do life without you." Through the evil one's enticement, they wanted to discover life, love, community, acceptance, significance, and purpose *outside* of a life-defining love relationship with God. They made a choice to live *independent* from God. They were now spiritually dead, separated from God, and lost. Theologians call Adam and Eve's cosmic rebellion *The Fall*. The apostle Paul says it this way in Romans 5:12, 17–21:

> Therefore, just as sin came into the world through one man, and death through sin, and so death spread to all men because all sinned.... For if, because of one man's trespass, death reigned through that one man, much more will those who receive the abundance of grace and the free gift of righteousness *reign* in life through the one man Jesus Christ. Therefore, as one trespass led to condemnation for all men, so one act of righteousness leads to justification and life for all men. For as by the one man's disobedience the many were made sinners, so by the one man's obedience the many will be made righteous. Now the law came in to increase the trespass, but where sin increased, *grace* abounded all the more, so that, *as* sin reigned in death, grace also might reign through righteousness leading to eternal life through Jesus Christ our Lord (esv).

Adam made a mess of things. Everything that you can think of or have experienced personally that is bad had its origin in the Garden of Eden. But let these inspiring words echo in your soul: Jesus, the Great Hero armed with "abundant grace," came to earth on a rescue mission to undo what Adam did.

HERO OR HIDER: THE CHOICE IS YOURS | Are you tired of hiding? If you are, the Great Hero is walking in your inner garden, calling your name. God did not say to Adam "Where are you?" because He did not know where Adam was. He's all-knowing and fully present everywhere (Psalm 139:7–12); of course He knew where Adam was hiding. He called out to Adam so that Adam could know *who He was* and that his Father still loved and pursued him despite his crime. And despite your sin, no matter how dark, God is calling your name. Sprint into the Great Hero's arms and receive a divine embrace of abundant grace.

Please stop putting on fig leaves and running behind the bushes like Adam to hide your sin. Come out of the darkness, into the marvelous light. He's calling your name. The hero's call to embrace "abundant grace" leads to an abundant life (John 10:10). God wants to cover your sin with the spiritual clothing He offers (Genesis 3:21). Does this mean there are no consequences for your sin? Of course not. Adam and Eve paid a steep price for their rebellion (Genesis 3:24), *but* their relationship with God was restored.

EMBRACING A THEOLOGY OF BROKENNESS | A doctor can only heal those who admit they are sick (Matthew 9:12). This is what Jesus meant when he said, "Blessed are the poor in spirit, for theirs is the kingdom of heaven" (Matthew 5:3 ESV). When we admit our brokenness to God, He begins to administer His grace to us. This is true for the non-Christ-follower *and* the Christ-follower. May the words of a hero named Peter encourage you:

> "Humble yourselves, therefore, under the mighty hand of God so that at the proper time he may exalt you, casting all your anxieties on him, because he cares for you" (1 Peter 5:6–7 ESV).

_____

A theology of brokenness. That goes against every fiber of my "natural" self. I want my mind to be transformed by God's Word to the point that I recognize brokenness as a good place to be...and even welcome it.

V. Gray

_____

The best day of your life will be the day that you approach God and say, "Here I am. Here's my anger, here's my addiction, here's my lust for power. God, here is all my stinky, rotten garbage. I am tired of hiding and covering myself in fig leaves; I am ready to be covered in grace. I'm ready to be a hero."

HEAD

- Read Genesis 3:1–24 and Romans 5:12, 17–20.
- Your sin does not cause God to run away from you; it moves His heart to run toward you so that you can embrace the grace that heals and transforms.
- Read Matthew 5:3 and embrace the "theology of brokenness."

HEART

- What are you feeling in your heart as you read today's entry? What are you hiding from God and those closest to you? This may be hard and painful, but rest assured, God's grace is a much better place than the spiritual trap you are currently in. Write down your feelings and prayers, asking God the Holy Spirit to help you embrace a "theology of brokenness" so you can receive grace and healing.

HANDS

- Read Romans 5:12, 15–20. Take a sheet of paper and draw a line down the middle. On the left side of the paper write "Adam" and on the right side of the paper write "Jesus." List what you received from Adam and then list what you received by having faith in Jesus.
- Every time you feel yourself wanting to hide or cover yourself in a fig leaf, say to yourself, "Run into the arms of the Great Hero's abundant grace." Daily reaffirm your need for His grace in your life!

THIRTEEN

HERO, DISCOVER YOUR TRUE SELF IN THE WILDERNESS

Then Jesus was led up by the Spirit into the wilderness to be tempted by the devil.
MATTHEW 4:1 ESV

FROM THE WATER TO THE WILDERNESS | In the garden, we lost our God-given identity.

In the wilderness, our God-given identity is restored and tested.

In Matthew 4, we find Jesus being led into the wilderness to be tempted by the evil one. This journey comes on the heels of Jesus' cousin John baptizing Him in the Jordan River. Jesus was baptized to *identify* with the human condition, not for his own sin. He is the sinless Lamb of God (John 1:29).

In the baptism scene, we hear the voice of God the Father say, "This is my beloved Son, with whom I am well pleased." And then we see the Holy Spirit in the form of a dove descending to rest on Jesus. This is awesome.

Next we find the Holy Spirit leading Jesus into the desert, or wilderness, to be tempted by the devil. Wait a second. Didn't God the Father just say that He loved Jesus? Why would God the Father have the Holy Spirit send His Son into the desert to be tempted by the devil? And not only was Jesus tempted, but he was tempted while in a weakened physical state because he had just spent forty days fasting.

EVERY MAN MUST ENTER THE WILDERNESS | God did this because heroes are forged in the desert's heat and by the evil one's tempting. God did this so you would not be surprised when you are led by the Spirit into the desert to be tempted by the evil one. In the desert's heat, and through the devil's tempting, you will have your God-given identity restored and tested.

THE THREE "P" WORDS | The evil one attacked and tempted Jesus with the three Ps: *power, prestige,* and *possessions.*[1] He will do the same to you. First, Satan tempted Jesus by appealing to Him to use His *power* to turn stones into bread (Matthew 4:3). Jesus could have used His divine power to do this. But if He did that, He would not have been able to understand your struggle with temptation (Hebrews 4:15), and you would not have the opportunity to learn how to have spiritual hand-to-hand combat with the forces of evil. Instead of using His divine power, Jesus quoted scripture and rested in His Father's power (Matthew 4:4).

Do not miss this: Jesus refused to establish His identity on the basis of what He could do. By Jesus refusing to use His divine power, He was telling Satan, "My identity is based in my Father's power, not Mine."

In what ways do the three "P" words show up in my life? I often "compete," instead of "complete" my husband. Lord, help me resist the temptation to define myself by my achievements and by the things the world says are valuable.

V. Gray

How many of you base your identity in what you do? Satan used this "P" on me for years. I thought my power, or my profession of being an NFL player, defined me. I thought people would accept me and like me because of what I did. Big problem: The NFL stands for *Not for Long*. If I lost my NFL career, who would I be? I bought the lie of believing that what I did defined me as a person. Do you feel that way? It's a terrible way to live, isn't it? It's terrible because when you anchor your identity in what you do, you never win. It's bondage. It's unheroic.

Second, Satan tempted Jesus by appealing to *prestige*. He invited Jesus to throw Himself from the top of the temple into the crowds below so they would immediately know that He was the Messiah (Matthew 4:5–6). Jesus knew it was not His time to reveal to the world that He was the Messiah, or Savior. His identity was founded not in opportunities to promote Himself, but in being God's Son. Jesus deflected Satan's appeal to prestige by quoting scripture (Matthew 4:7).

The evil one is going to tempt *you* with prestige, as well. We live in the age of self-preoccupation; psychologists call this *narcissism* and *self-promotion*. Everyone wants to be a superstar. One of the reasons Facebook, MySpace, YouTube, and reality shows have exploded in growth is because people can now promote themselves. (I pray that we use these technologies in healthy ways, not in soul-destroying ways.)

Our culture values and worships superstars.

Jesus valued humility and called His followers to be servants (John 13:1–17)!

Third, Satan tempted Jesus by appealing to *possessions*. He offered Jesus all the kingdoms of the world (Matthew 4.8–9). Jesus, secure and grounded in His identity as God's Son, refused to find His identity in possessions. He crushed Satan once again by using scripture (Matthew 4:10).

The forces of evil will tempt you this way, as well. In America, it is the number one scheme that the evil one uses to shipwreck lives. Every commercial screams at the top of its lungs: "If you do not buy this product, you are worthless! By buying this product...you are somebody." There is nothing wrong with having nice things. But it is terribly wrong when nice things have and define you. It is terribly wrong when your identity is found in what you possess. Your possessions will begin to possess you. You will never have enough. You will spend countless hours pursuing something that is unattainable. You will be on a quest for what matters least, while neglecting what matters most—God and people. This is an unheroic life. This is sad.

STRENGTH TRAINING IN THE WILDERNESS | Jesus knew His identity was secure and anchored as God's Son. He resisted and drop-kicked the devil in the face by refusing to find his identity in power, prestige, or possessions. Hero-in-the-making, you, too, can resist and defeat the evil one, because you are God's child by your faith in Jesus (John 1:12; 1 John 3:2).

HEAD

- ❧ Satan wants you to find your identity in your own power, prestige, and possessions. This will ruin your life.
- ❧ God has created you to find your identity as His child. This will bless your life. And you will bless others.
- ❧ Reread Matthew 4:1–11, John 1:12, and 1 John 3:2.

HEART

- ❧ What feelings are being stirred in you as you read today's entry? Are you in the wilderness being tempted? How is Satan using power, prestige, and possessions to pull you away from God? Describe how that is being played out in your life. Write down your feelings and ask God to empower you to work through them.

HANDS

- ❧ Send yourself a text three times today saying, "Power, prestige, and possessions do not define me; being God's child does." If you don't text, write it on a three-by-five note card and look at it three times today.
- ❧ Write as your status in Facebook or Twitter: Through Jesus, I am defined by being God's child.

FOURTEEN

HERO, YOU ARE ALIVE

But God, being rich in mercy, because of the great love with which he loved us,
even when we were dead in our trespasses, made us alive together with Christ—
by grace you have been saved.

Ephesians 2:4–5 ESV

WHAT WOULD IT BE LIKE? | What would it be like to live like Jesus for a day? What would it be like to love people and creation like He does? To worship God the Father…to live in complete dependency on the Holy Spirit…to humbly serve hurting people…like Jesus did?

What if the *eternal kind of life* that Jesus invites all of humanity to experience is more than a trip to heaven when we die? What if His invitation is really an invitation to live from His awe-inspiring life? What if Jesus is freely offering humanity the joy of possessing His eternal, all-sufficient, all-satisfying, God-glorifying life *right now*?

What if the thoughts of Jesus, the desires of Jesus, the will of Jesus, the faith of Jesus, the love of Jesus, the generosity of Jesus, the mission of Jesus, the humility of Jesus, could be expressed through you? What if Galatians 2:20 were actually true?…

> My old self has been crucified with Christ. It is no longer I who live,
> but Christ lives in me. So I live in this earthly body by trusting in the
> Son of God, who loved me and gave himself for me (NLT).

The Great Hero has come to live in and through you. You have been created to be His sacred outlet for His heroic life to express itself!

THE GOAL | Contrary to popular—and unbiblical—belief, God's greatest goal for your life is not *comfort*, but *character formation*. Think about it. If all Jesus came to do was die for your sins so you could go to heaven when you die, then he would have taken you to heaven the nanosecond you trusted in Him to forgive your sins. Salvation is bigger than that selfish understanding of the Gospel. It is true that Jesus died to forgive all your sins. It is equally true that He rose from the dead to infuse you with His resurrected life so you can begin moment by moment to reflect Him to the world. And by steadily, and progressively, reflecting Him, you become a source of good to the world, like Jesus.

This slow and steady process is described several ways in the Bible:

For those whom he foreknew he also *predestined* to be conformed to the image of his Son, in order that he might be the firstborn among many brothers (Romans 8:29 ESV).

My little children, *for* whom I am again in the anguish of childbirth until Christ is formed in you! (Galatians 4:19 ESV).

And we all, with unveiled face, beholding the glory of the Lord, are being transformed into the same image from one degree of glory to another. For this comes from the Lord who is the Spirit (2 Corinthians 3:18 ESV).

Until we all attain to the unity of the faith and of the knowledge of the Son of God, to mature manhood, to the measure of the stature of the fullness of Christ (Ephesians 4:13 ESV).

The Great Hero's highest goal for you is the formation of Christ in you. Out of an infinite ocean of mercy, God made you alive *in* Christ through grace, so that by grace and in grace, Jesus can be formed in you. What's your role? Your role in this transformation project is to surrender your will to His (Romans 6:11–13).

MORE THAN MORALISTIC RELIGION | We must never confuse biblical Christ-following with moralism. Because you are made in the image of God, you can do "horizontal good works" and develop strong moral character. *But you can never live the life of Christ unless the life of Christ is living in you.* God is not interested in you finding ways to keep your sin under control. He wants you to live from the life of Christ because your "life is hidden with Christ in God" (Colossians 3:3 ESV)! This produces something far greater and more heroic than mere moralism. Think of it this way: Moralism is like a field with no weeds. A life lived from the life of Jesus is like a field with no weeds and a beautiful array of vibrant, scent-filled flowers displaying their beauty.

––––––––––

I don't want my family to think I am just a very good person—I want them to see something supernatural in me. I don't want to raise my children to be externally compliant—I want them to experience the Christ-life: to be the field with the beautiful flowers!

––––––––––

V. Gray

NO ONE CAN—BUT JESUS | No one can live the Christian life…except Jesus. The sooner you realize this liberating truth, the sooner you will be daily transformed into the image of Christ. Jesus *gave* His life for you, so that He could *give* His life to you, so that He could *live* His life through you.[1]

The more you surrender your will to His and allow Jesus to live through you, the more you will do good to family, friends, and the world. That's a faith people will be attracted to. That's a heroic life.

HEAD

- Slowly and prayerfully read Ephesians 2:1–10, Galatians 2:20, Romans 8:29, and Galatians 4:19.
- God's goal for you is not your comfort, but the transformation of your character into Christlikeness.
- You are the sacred outlet through which Jesus expresses His heroic life. Embrace and surrender to that reality.

HEART

❧   What feelings are you experiencing as you read today's entry? Do not rush through this. Reread the chapter if you need to. Let God deal with you. It's worth it. Write about your feelings and ask God the Holy Spirit to help you embrace the Jesus-forming work He wants to do in your life.

HANDS

❧   Ask God the Holy Spirit to place three people on your mind to share what you've learned and experienced from this entry.

FIFTEEN

HERO, YOU ARE WEARING A NEW SUIT

You were all baptized into Christ, and so you were all clothed with Christ.
GALATIANS 3:27 NCV

I LOVE SUITS | I grew up poor, wearing hand-me-down clothes. After seeing the movie *Trading Places*, I figured I could have a nice suit one day like Eddie Murphy's character Billy Ray Valentine. Valentine was a poor street bum who was taken in by some Chicago businessmen conducting an experiment that involved giving him a new job, some money, and some nice suits. When he got the job, the money, and the suits, he changed. As a little boy, it was etched into my heart that if I had a nice suit, I'd made it.

During my NFL career, I developed an obsession with suits. I even had my own tailor to custom-make my suits. My favorite one was all-white. I unleashed it for the first game of the 1997 season when we, the Indianapolis Colts, traveled down to Florida to play the Miami Dolphins. This suit was so sweet that when I entered the airport and my teammates saw me, they all gasped.

When I wore these sweet threads, everything about me changed. I began to walk like John Travolta in *Staying Alive*. I began to talk like James Bond 007. And if I saw *anything* that would mess up my suit, I'd avoid it like a deer avoids a mountain lion. This suit made me feel and look like I was somebody.

When I looked in the mirror while wearing this suit, I did not see a poor boy from the ghetto; I saw a man that had made it. I was wrong, of course. My suit on the outside may have looked good, but my spiritual suit on the inside was naked.

Here's the soul-tattoo: *When you decide to follow Jesus, He gives you a new spiritual suit.*

You were all baptized into Christ, and so you were all clothed with Christ (Galatians 3:27 NCV).

THE JESUS SUIT | In the context of Galatians 3:27, to be baptized into Christ means to identify with Him. When I played for the Colts, I wore a Colts uniform to identify with the team. When I played for the Carolina Panthers, I wore a Panthers jersey to identify with the Panthers' team. When you trust Jesus to be your rescuer, He gives you His "suit of righteousness." Theologians call this the doctrine of *justification*. I call this Good News!

God is perfectly righteous. You and I and the rest of humanity are not (Romans 3:10). God can only be face-to-face with perfectly righteous people. So what does He do about this problem? Let your mind marinate in the greatness of the Great Hero. He does not excuse our sin, nor does He loosen His standards. God doesn't just ignore our mutiny, nor does He ease up on His righteous demands. Instead of dismissing our sin, Jesus becomes our sin and is executed in our place! God's holiness is honored. Our sin is punished and condemned, and we are saved (Romans 5:8–9).

Jesus does what we could never do, so we can become what we never thought was possible: Being perfectly righteous before a perfectly righteous God (Hebrews 10:14).

I want the reality of wearing the Jesus-suit to sink in and provide proper perspective to all areas of my life—what others think of me, how I think of me, and what I believe God thinks of me. This anchors my soul in truth.

V. Gray

Jesus exchanges His perfect righteousness for our unrighteousness. Jesus takes off His righteous suit and gives it to us as a free gift (Romans 5:17). Paul says it this way:

God made him who had no sin to be sin for us, so that in him we might become the righteousness of God (2 Corinthians 5:21 NIV).

UPWARD, INWARD, OUTWARD | *Upward*. The doctrine of justification means that God has not only forgiven your sins, but He also now sees you as perfectly righteous in Christ. He is completely pleased with you because Jesus' suit of righteousness infuses your entire being.

I know…it's hard to believe, isn't it? That's why grace is so amazing. That's why Paul says:

Indeed, I count everything as loss because of the surpassing worth of knowing Christ Jesus my Lord. For his sake I have suffered the loss of all things and count them as rubbish, in order that I may gain Christ and be found in him, not having a righteousness of my own that comes from the law, but that which comes through faith in Christ, the righteousness from God that depends on faith (Philippians 3:8–9 ESV).

Inward. A man will always live accordingly to how he sees himself. Justification means that we can now see ourselves as righteous because we are wearing Jesus' suit of righteousness. I tried to avoid anything that would make my white suit dirty. Why? Because I loved being clean. The more you embrace, meditate on, and marinate in the reality of the Jesus-suit you are wearing, the more your life will reflect Jesus. You will find yourself thinking, "I'm wearing the Jesus-suit; why would I want to watch porn?" "I'm wearing the Jesus-suit; why would I want to backstab my coworker?" "I'm wearing the Jesus-suit; why would I have sex with my girlfriend?"

Faith is believing what God says is true. He says you are perfectly righteous in Jesus. Do you believe Him? The battle will wage in your soul like a ship at sea in the midst of a violent storm. If you drop your anchor, the storm may toss you, but you will not capsize.

Outward. As Jesus' suit of righteousness fits you more comfortably, you will begin to extend grace and forgiveness to those who betray, hurt, and lie to you. A hero is a man that has the God-generated ability to unconditionally love another human being even after being let down, disappointed, or wounded by them. That's a heroic love.

This is the life you were created for. It's easy to have sentimental love when people love you back. True love is realized in the reality of great disappointment. Just like Jesus, He loved you…even when you disappointed Him (Romans 5:8–9). Because you are wearing the Jesus-suit, you now have power to do likewise. Be a hero today and wear your Jesus-suit with style.

HEAD

- Meditate on 2 Corinthians 5:21, Galatians 3:27, and Philippians 3:8–9.
- The doctrine of justification means that God has not only forgiven your sins, but He also now sees you as perfectly righteous in Christ. He is completely satisfied with you because Jesus' suit of righteousness covers your entire being.

HEART

- What are you feeling as you read today's entry? Is it hard to believe that God sees you as perfectly righteous? Why? Write down your feelings and ask God the Holy Spirit to anchor this reality in your life. This will be hard. The evil one will assault you with every sin from your past, present, and future. Always sprint back to what Jesus has done for you on your behalf.

HANDS

- I want you to preach the Gospel to yourself. Remind yourself as often as possible that you are wearing the Jesus-suit.
- Write someone close to you a letter explaining the doctrine of justification and the practical implications it has on your life.

SIXTEEN

HERO, GOD KILLED HIS SON TO BE YOUR FRIEND

The greatest love a person can show is to die for his friends.
JOHN 15:13 NCV

GOD WANTS TO BE YOUR FRIEND | God killed His Son to be your friend. For the Christ-follower reading this, slow down and let this deep truth ground itself like anchor in your soul. For the non-follower of Christ, ask God to reveal this truth and empower you to embrace it. Set your heart on this verse:

> But it was the Lord who decided to crush him and make him suffer. The Lord made his life a penalty offering (Isaiah 53:10 NCV).

GOD KILLED HIS SON SO YOU COULD BE HIS FRIEND | The Great Hero hungers to be a great friend to you. In the words of my teenage daughter, Presley, "God wants to be your BFF" (Best Friend Forever). Your friendship with God will define all your other friendships. A great friendship with God produces great friendships with yourself and others. A poor friendship with God produces poor friendships with yourself and others.

HUGE PROBLEM | Because of Adam's betrayal in the Garden of Eden, we inherited a type of virus called sin (Romans 5:12). Have you ever heard of a "crack baby?" "Crack babies" are born addicted to "crack" cocaine because their mothers used it during the pregnancy. Just as a "crack baby" is born corrupted and addicted to a toxic drug, you and me and the rest of humanity are all corrupted by and addicted to sin (Isaiah 53:6; Ephesians 2:1–3). Theologians call this the doctrine of *original sin*. Sin simply means "missing the mark." This word refers to humanity's inability to be what God desires us to be. It speaks of our failure to live in perfect harmony with God and others. We are sinners by nature and by action. That's the bad news.

Have you ever wondered why little children must be taught to tell the truth, to share, and to be kind? Why don't we have to teach them to be selfish, unkind, and lie? Because of original sin. Why is our world a mess? Original sin.

MORE BAD NEWS | This bad news gets worse. Not only does our original sin separate us from God, but it also makes us His enemies. Listen to Paul, the apostle:

> While we were God's enemies, he made us his friends through the death of his Son. Surely, now that we are his friends, he will save us through his Son's life (Romans 5:10 NCV).

These words of truth are abrasive and ugly to our postmodern ears. How can I be God's enemy? He loves everyone, right? Just as Jesus told us to love our enemies, God loves His enemies (John 3:16–21). God in Christ is on a mission to turn enemies into friends:

> "All this is from God, who reconciled us to himself through Christ and gave us the ministry of reconciliation: that God was reconciling the world to himself in Christ, not counting men's sins against them. And he has committed to us the message of reconciliation" (2 Corinthians 5:19 NCV).

Because God loves relentlessly, pursues passionately, and is eternally holy, He must release His wrath on sin and exile sin from His presence. Any other God would not be worth worshiping. Think of it this way: If a terrible disease began to spread from one person to another, killing all in its path, it would be unloving to not isolate the diseased people from the others who have yet to contract the life-ending disease. The disease is an enemy that must be destroyed.

Out of His great love and mercy, God sends Jesus to destroy the enemy called sin (Colossians 2:13–15). He destroys it by taking the enemy sin upon Himself so that we will not be held under God's wrath and be eternally exiled from God's holy presence. This is an act of sheer grace. As the old hymn says, "Nothing in my hands I bring, simply to the cross I cling."

FRIEND OF GOD | *Upward.* The word *reconciliation* means that at one time you were a hostile enemy of God, separated from Him. In the Bible, this is called spiritual death. If you remain an enemy of God, you will be spiritually dead in this life and estranged or separated from God in hell in the next (2 Thessalonians 1:8-9). And you know what? It breaks God's heart when people reject Him and choose to spend eternity away from Him (Ezekiel 18:23; 2 Peter 3:9).

Here's the good news: If you've put your faith in Jesus, you are now God's friend. You are totally accepted by God. The Great Hero is your friend. He accepts you. And His friendship and acceptance of you is based on His abundant grace, not on your self-effort to appease Him by trying to do good (Titus 3:4–7). Friends, embracing and integrating this truth in your life will forever change you.

Inward. America does not need self-esteem. We need a heavy dose of God-esteem! Self-esteem is nothing more than the Adam and Eve syndrome that got us into the mess we are in now. Self-esteem means finding your identity and value in being *independent* of God. God-esteem means that your value and identity is dependent on being God's beloved child and friend.

Being a wife and a mother is a hard calling, especially in a culture that values self-esteem. To be who I was created to be, I must be anchored in God-esteem. I must find my worth in who God says I am and encourage my family to do the same.

V. Gray

For a long time I did not like being me. I stuttered, so people made fun of me. My father left me, so I felt unlovable. When your identity and value is found in self-esteem, you try to improve yourself. This is a fruitless adventure that leads to the sabotaging of relationships. You end relationships before it's discovered that you are not perfect and someone has the chance to abandon you. I couldn't learn to be my own friend until I realized that God was my friend and only He could improve me. Then I began to like being Derwin.

A few years ago my family and I were swimming at the YMCA. A couple of teenage boys noticed me. As they begin to walk toward me, I immediately thought they must be remembering me from my football days with the Carolina Panthers. *They must want my autograph,* I thought to myself. To my surprise, they asked if my name was Stephen Davis, the top running back for the Panthers. I said "No." They walked away.

Before shame and rejection could overcome me, I said, "I love being Derwin. Being God's friend is enough for me." The more you become secure in being God's friend, the greater capacity you have for friendship with yourself and others. Is this easy? No! It is a constant battle to set my eyes on Jesus, my Best Friend Forever, in the midst of constant soul-distraction.

Outward. Who are your friends? I'm not talking about guys you have superficial relationships with that revolve around common interests or your job. I'm talking about real friends—the kind of friends that will help you construct yourself into a man of honor, sacrifice, integrity, fierce love, and wisdom, not false friends that will help you deconstruct your life.

Few people have real friends. Few people are willing to *be* real with God, themselves, and others. Real friends inspire each other to live heroic lives (Hebrews 3:13). They are secure enough in being God's friend that they are willing to ask the tough questions. They are also willing to be asked the tough questions and to be challenged. They are willing to rebuke each other (Proverbs 17:10, 27:6). They are willing to work through conflict instead of running from conflict. My best friends have been the ones that love me enough to tell me the truth, even when I did not want to hear it. It wasn't what I wanted to hear, but it was what I needed to hear. *Have that kind of friend and be that kind of friend.*

HEAD

- God killed His Son to be your friend. Read Isaiah 53:10.
- Prayerfully read Romans 5:10 and 2 Corinthians 5:19.
- God wants to be your BFF! Cultivate God-esteem, not self-esteem.

HEART

- Are you God's friend through faith in His Son Jesus? If not, embrace His friendship through faith in His Son. In your own language say to the Great Hero, "Today I choose to receive your invitation of life, forgiveness, and friendship through Your Son Jesus. I am ready to follow You. Teach me what it means to be Your disciple and a member of Your family called the Church. Amen." Let someone that is a Christ-follower know of your decision to become a friend of Jesus.
- What feelings are being triggered in you as you read today's entry? Take some time to reflect on what you've read. Do not rush. Cultivate the discipline of holy listening and silence. Write down your feelings and ask God to empower you to work through them.

HANDS

- According to what you have just read, write down what a real friend is.
- Write down the names of your real friends.
- To whom are you a real friend?
- Pray and ask the Great Hero to bring real friends into your life and that you would become a real friend.

SEVENTEEN

HERO, YOU ARE NOT WHO YOU USED TO BE

Therefore, if anyone is in Christ, he is a new creation.
The old has passed away; behold, the new has come.

2 CORINTHIANS 5:17 ESV

DELETE | I love the DELETE button on my computer. If I mess up, I can just delete it. Don't you wish life could be that way? But because life does not work that way, many of you live with a thousand-pound anchor in your soul called regret and shame. The regret and shame from your past shapes how you interact with God, yourself, people, and life's circumstances. It influences the jobs you pursue, the relationships you pursue, and the people you surround yourself with.

DESMOND'S STORY | For several years I pastored a man who I'll call Desmond. He was sexually abused by an older teenage boy for many years beginning when he was nine years old. He also was verbally abused by his alcoholic father. As a result of these traumatic experiences, shame and regret grew like a wild weed in his heart. To numb the pain, Desmond began to drink heavily and engage in promiscuous sexual activity with men and women. The more he did these things, the more he felt regret and shame suffocating his soul. Shame and regret is fertile soil for addiction.

As a Christ-follower, Desmond struggled deeply and painfully with how God could love him in light of his alcoholism and sexually promiscuous lifestyle. "How could a woman ever want a man that was sexually molested and now has sex with other men?" he asked. How could other Christians ever accept someone like him?

Desmond wished he could just press the DELETE button on these aspects of his life. But he couldn't.

BEFORE YOU CONDEMN | Before you pick up your rocks to stone and condemn Desmond, how do you deal with regret and shame? How do you numb the pain?

Maybe you numb it with food.

Maybe in being a super fan of your favorite sports team.

Maybe it's video game addiction.

Maybe it's your job. Are you the first one there and the last one to leave? Is seventy hours a week no big deal for you?

Maybe it's in people-pleasing and doing a bunch of stuff at your church so people will see you as a super-Christian...while on the inside, your soul is cold and dying.

Maybe it's pornography addiction. For my female readers, if your husband is physically capable but avoids having sex with you, I strongly suggest, based on a decade of men's ministry experience, that he's most likely trapped in porn addiction.

Maybe it's prescription drug addiction. Of course, you justify this drug addiction because it is prescribed to you by your doctor. This is a much more respectable addiction than the fifteen-year-old prostitute that is hooked on crack, isn't it?

So before we condemn Desmond, let us remember we need the same grace he does. Desmond reminds me of a man in the Bible named Matthew. Let's look at his story.

FROM ZERO TO HERO | Why would Jesus ask Matthew to follow Him (Matthew 9:9)? This man was a seriously messed-up Jew! He betrayed his people by working for the spiritually unclean Roman occupiers, taking tax money from his people. His religiously committed Jewish brothers would have seen him as a shameful man in a shameful profession and as a disgusting traitor (Matthew 11:19).

Matthew was not just any tax collector. He was a rich port tax collector. Because of the diversity of goods flowing into Capernaum where he worked, he had the power to tax the goods coming in there more excessively than the tax collectors who worked on the land. This job made him lower than dirt in the eyes of many religiously committed Jews. His betrayal was so bad that some rabbis taught that port tax collectors like Matthew could never be forgiven by God! For a moment, think about the regret and shame that must have been stored up in his heart.

Jesus, being the Great Hero clothed in humanity, is always looking for those filled with shame and regret. He set His sights on Matthew. He asked Matthew to follow Him and to become His student in the school of living. This was a big deal in the Jewish culture. To have a rabbi ask you to follow him was an honor. And no Jewish rabbi would ask a moral screw-up like Matthew to follow him unless that rabbi was Jesus.

Can you imagine the emotions that Matthew must have felt when Jesus asked him to become His disciple? It would be as if Jesus pressed the DELETE button and said, "Matthew, all your sin, shame, and regret I have deleted. You are not who you used to be; you are now a new man because you are in a life-defining love relationship with Me."

Let the Great Hero's grace wash over me like a refreshing waterfall on a hot day—a grace that remembers my sins no more. In that reality, I am empowered to shower others with His love, grace, and forgiveness— and that's living a heroic life!

V. Gray

PARTY TIME | Matthew's encounter with Jesus forever changes him. He throws a party for his sinner friends and invites Jesus to hang out (Luke 5:29–32). Don't you find it interesting that Matthew threw a party to celebrate His new life and invited his sinner friends to this party so they could meet Jesus, the giver of new life? When was the last time you've been this excited about your new life in Jesus?

The religious people got mad at Jesus for associating with sinners. But why wouldn't Jesus go to Matthew's party full of sinners? He's the soul-physician! His grace is the medicine that cures sinners and makes them new. Jesus made Matthew a new person. Theologians call this *regeneration*. Sinners like me and Desmond call this Good News (2 Corinthians 5:17)!

Upward. Because of your participation in Jesus' life by faith in Him, you have been infused with Jesus' very life. You are a new person. The Great Hero Himself, the Father (James 1:18), the Son (John 5:21), and the Holy Spirit (Titus 3:5) all play a role in your regeneration.

Inward. Your constant spiritual battle will be in your believing that you are a new person despite not feeling and acting like one at times. Please hear this with your soul: *Your past sin, regret, and shame no longer define you. You are not who you used to be.* There are times I am bombarded with the ugly things from my past. And sometimes I will say out loud, "I remember the ugly things of my past, but more importantly, I remember the beautiful thing Jesus did on my behalf to make me new!"

Because you are a new person in Jesus, you can live with Jesus-centered confidence, courage, and joy that is not based on your circumstances but in the immovable, undiminishing love and mission of Jesus.

Outward. Because you are new in Jesus, regret and shame can no longer limit you. Risk and try things for God's glory that you never thought were possible. Maybe it's a job. Maybe it's becoming vulnerable to your wife. Only you know what it is. Life is short, so in the words of Rocky Balboa, my wife's childhood crush, "Go for it." Be the hero you were created to be!

CELEBRATION | When Desmond got married, he invited all his sinner friends to the wedding to see how Jesus can delete an old life and create a new heroic one.

HEAD

- Reread 2 Corinthians 5:17.
- You are a new person in Christ. Jesus' life now pulsates in and through you. You are not who you used to be.

HEART

- What feelings are rising up in you as you read today's entry? What have the emotions of regret and shame done to your life? What things are you doing to avoid feeling them? Take some time to reflect on what you've read. Write down your feelings and ask God to empower you to work through them.

HANDS

- Write down the things you have done that have given you regret and shame.
- Next take a red marker and draw a huge cross in the center of the paper.
- Then cross out those things that you have done that are now covered over by Christ.
- At the top of the page, write "I am a New Man in Jesus, Capable of Being a Hero."

EIGHTEEN

HERO, GOD IS NOT MAD AT YOU

*He is the propitiation for our sins, and not for ours only
but also for the sins of the whole world.*

1 JOHN 2:2 ESV

TWO GOATS, SOME BLOOD, AND A CLIFF | *Upward.* God is not mad at you. Let's dive *heart* first into a great mystery called the Day of Atonement. In Leviticus 16 we see what took place on this sacred day. In obedience to God's command, the high priest chose two goats without defect. The goats represented sinless perfection. One was called the "scapegoat." The high priest placed his hands on the head of the scapegoat and confessed the nation of Israel's sin upon it, and then it was released into the wilderness. This act signified the removal of sin so that the nation of Israel was free from God's wrath and judgment against its sin for a year.

Sometimes the scapegoat would find its way back to the camp. This was bad news for the people because it was like their sins were coming back on them. According to some sources, if this happened, someone would then lead the goat to a cliff in the wilderness and push it over, making sure the goat did not return to the camp. This was a physical act that represented this reality, "He has taken our sins away from us as far as the east is from west" (Psalm 103:12 NCV). This is called the doctrine of *expiation.*

The other goat that had been selected was sacrificed, and its blood was taken by the high priest into the Holy of Holies, the innermost part of the Temple where the Ark of the Covenant was located. On top of the Ark was the mercy seat, essentially God's throne on earth where man met God

(Exodus 25:21–22). Hovering above the mercy seat was a cloud of smoke that represented God's presence. The high priest would take the blood of the sacrificed goat and sprinkle it over the mercy seat, which contained the Ten Commandments (Exodus 25:16, 21).

Let's gather ourselves. So we have God's presence hovering above, symbolizing God looking down on the mercy seat. And when the high priest covered the mercy seat with the goat's blood, it covered over, or atoned, for the people's sin (Hebrews 9:1–7). So now when God looks down, He sees the blood of the goat covering the Ten Commandments, which have been violated by the people. This act of grace means that God's anger was satisfied, or propitiated, by the sacrificed goat's blood.

Why all the blood? Great question. God connects sin and blood to reveal that sin results in spiritual death (Romans 6:23). The goat's blood also represents life given as payment for sin. Can you see the work of Jesus in this ancient practice? Marinate in the certainty of these verses:

> Behold the Lamb of God who takes away the sin of the world (John 1:29 ESV).

> He is the propitiation for our sins, and not for ours only but also for the sins of the whole world (1 John 2:2 ESV).

> Since, therefore, we have now been justified by his blood, much more shall we be saved by him from the wrath of God (Romans 5:9 ESV).

Theologians call this the doctrine of propitiation. I call it the Good News. *Propitiation* means that by Jesus' death on the cross in humanity's place, He alone has satisfied God's wrath. In light of this truth, you are deeply loved by God. Rest your soul in 1 John 4:9–10:

> In this the love of God was made manifest among us, that God sent his only Son into the world, so that we might live through him. In this is love, *not* that we have loved God but that he loved us and sent his Son to be the propitiation for our sins (ESV).

As you personally take hold of Jesus' life, God is no longer angry with you. Have you placed yourself in Christ by embracing His sacrifice on your behalf? If you have not, do it right now. Receive Him into your life by confessing that He lived the perfect life you could never live. That he died on the cross in your place to satisfy God's wrath. And that He rose from the dead to now take up residence in your life and adopt you into His family called the Church. If you believe this, you are in Christ. Welcome home!

DISCIPLINE OUT OF LOVE | Please understand, just as I discipline my son out of love when he acts up, the Great Hero will discipline you as well (Hebrews 12:7). The Good News is that you are no longer under His wrath or anger.

Inward. If you believe that God is angry with you, you are going to be angry with yourself. If you think you have to clean yourself up and please God by your behavior, then two negative things will happen. First, if you succeed with behavior modification, you will become a self-righteous jerk that no one wants to be around. Second, you will become so frustrated when you let God down that you will give up. Either way, you lose; and all the people you have a relationship with will suffer, too.

The self-righteous religious person is no closer to God then the self-loathing non-religious person. Both are lost. Both are unheroic. God's love and acceptance of me is not based on me trying to behave better so God won't zap me from heaven. It is based on Jesus' sinless life, sacrificial death, and glorious resurrection. And you know what's so amazing about grace? The more I rest in His work on my behalf, the more I desire to do good (Titus 2:11–14). But the more I focus on self-improvement, the more I sin and get frustrated. No one wonder Paul said "Set your mind on things above, not on earthly things. For your life is now hidden with Christ in God" (Colossians 3:2–3). Is it easy setting our minds on Jesus? No! But is it worth it? Yes.

———

If God is not angry at me, then I dont need to be angry at myself or with others. What a freeing truth! This can only be accomplished by the Holy Spirits power in me. Thank You, Lord, that You and You alone make this possible!

V. Gray

———

Outward. I was able to release my anger toward my father because I partnered with the Holy Spirit to apply this doctrine to my life. Several years ago, I was sitting at my computer writing letters to my family and friends. I was going on and on about how awesome Jesus was. Then I heard a voice. The voice said, "Find your father." I said, "No," accompanied by a few curse words. Finally I gave in to the unrelenting voice. The impression from God that I received was this: "Derwin, I forgave you, even when you hurt me. I forgave you so you could forgive him. Release that anger, son."

After several days of wrestling with God, I connected with my father. I told him that I loved him, forgave him, and wanted him to be involved in my family's life. And for the first time in my life, I heard my father say, "Son, thank you for forgiving me. I love you."

HEAD

❧ Reread John 1:29, 1 John 2:2, Romans 5:9, Psalm 103:12.
❧ Propitiation means that by Jesus' death on the cross in humanity's place, He alone has satisfied God's wrath. In light of this truth, you are deeply loved by God.

HEART

❧ What feelings are being stirred in you as you read today's entry? Reflect for several moments before you write anything. Take some time to orient yourself Godward so you can hear from Him. Write down your feelings and ask God to empower you to work through them.
❧ Is it hard for you to believe that God is not angry with you?

HANDS

❧ Unforgiveness and anger are like drinking poison and hoping the person you are mad at will die. Today, do the heroic thing by trusting in the indwelling life of Jesus within you to forgive them, or yourself, and be set free. You know the drill: Make that phone call or write that letter.
❧ Memorize 1 John 2:2 and Romans 5:9.

NINETEEN

HERO, YOU ARE NO LONGER A SLAVE

We know that our old self was crucified with him in order that
the body of sin might be brought to nothing, so that we
would no longer be enslaved to sin.

ROMANS 6:6 ESV

ROOTS | I'll never forget the first time I saw the movie *Roots*. This 12-hour miniseries based on the novel by the same name and authored by Alex Haley chronicled the lives of African slaves in America. As a child, it was hard for me to believe that other people would enslave and treat another group of people so inhumanely. I had no mental grid for what I was watching, and my heart could not deal with the emotions I was experiencing.

I would daydream about what it would have been like to be a slave who was placed on the auction block and offered for sale. I would see myself as a little boy being ripped away from my grandmother as I was sold to a new master on a new plantation.

REDEMPTION | In the movie, people are kidnapped from their villages in Africa, taken across the Atlantic Ocean by ship in subhuman conditions, held in bondage, and forced to be slaves. He or she was then put on the auction block and offered for sale. The more valuable the slave, the higher the price. In biblical times, there were slaves as well. Israel was one of many nations under Roman occupation. Some people were also made slaves because of their inability to pay their debts. In these cases, as in those of African slaves, if someone wanted to free a slave, he had to pay the redemption price or ransom for the slave.

KIDNAP AND RANSOM | Through the sin of Adam, the father of the human race, you and I were kidnapped by sin and Satan, and we were being held as slaves until the price was paid to set us free. You see, friends, slavery is alive and thriving on planet Earth. All humans are born enslaved to sin and to Satan. And there is nothing we can do to set ourselves free. Someone stronger must come and rescue us. Someone must walk to the slave auction block and purchase our freedom. Only *One* is rich enough in grace and mercy to pay the ransom price for humanity. His name is Jesus.

> The Son of Man came not to be served but to serve, and to give his life as a ransom for many (Matthew 20:28 ESV).

> You are not your own, for you were bought with a price. So glorify God in your body (1 Corinthians 6:19–20 ESV).

Jesus bought you. Not with money, silver, or gold—He bought you with His life! Do you know who He paid? Not Satan, but God. Jesus bought you so you could be free from the chains of sin that prevent you from living a heroic life. He bought you so you could live as a free man. What does that mean? Let's find out.

Upward. Every summer in Texas, many African-Americans celebrate *Juneteenth.* This celebration dates back to June 19, 1865, when Major General Gordon Granger landed in Galveston, Texas. He and his Union soldiers arrived with the good news that the Civil War had ended and that the slaves were now free. Did you catch the date of when he arrived? This good news came two and a half years after President Lincoln's Emancipation Proclamation—which had become official on January 1, 1863. The slaves in Texas had been free for more than two years, but they didn't even know it!

Here's the deal: Satan wants you to be ignorant of the fact that when Jesus purchased you, you, too, were set free from sin, death, and Satan. In Romans 6:1–10, Paul asks a life-transforming question: "Do you not know?" In essence, he is asking:

> Do you not know that when Jesus died on the cross, supernaturally you died with Him?

Do you not know that the sin nature you inherited from Adam has been executed on the cross and you are now pulsating with Jesus' resurrection life?

Do you not know that Jesus' resurrection life now rules and reigns in you?

Satan wants you to live like a slave even though Jesus has bought your freedom. Satan wants you to keep believing that salvation is only a trip to heaven when you die.

You must remember you are now alive and free in Jesus. You are dead to sin, the nature inherited from Adam. Hero-in-the-making, the Great Hero lives in you. You are no longer defined by Adam's life, but that of Jesus. Embrace Him.

Inward. You must reckon or hold firmly like a bulldog to this reality: You are dead to the Adam-life and alive to God through the Jesus-life (Romans 6:11).

During my NFL career, I learned that emotions cannot carry you through an entire game. What carries you through is a mind committed to the game plan. The better I knew and trusted the game plan, the more effective I would play despite pain, stress, and physical exhaustion. This is equally true of following Jesus; you must be committed to the reality that through faith in Jesus you are *dead to the Adam-life and alive to God through the Jesus-life.*

Our world would have us believe that we are free, especially in America. And maybe we are free politically, but we are not truly living in freedom at the core of our beings. I want to be saturated with the truth that I am free to live a life that pleases the Lord.

V. Gray

Outward. Finally, you must surrender your will to Jesus' life within you (Romans 6:11–13). You must choose to believe that you are alive to God in Christ and that you are no longer in slavery to sin. You must choose, moment by moment, to say, "Jesus, Your will be done, not mine." Even though at your deepest level you are alive in Christ, you must still battle your flesh. Your flesh is your desires that are contrary to Jesus' way of life (Galatians 5:19–21).

When you sin—and, Christ-follower, you will—thank God for His continual forgiveness (Ephesians 1:7). Then choose to walk in His power.

You can "present yourself to God as those who have been brought from death to life, and your members to God as instruments for righteousness" (Romans 6:13 ESV). The word *instrument* means *weapon*. Hero-in-the-making, you are a weapon of grace in God's mighty and majestic hand.

FREE AT LAST, FREE AT LAST | You are no longer a slave because you are under grace, not a set of external religious rules (Romans 6:14). Grace is God Himself in the Person of Jesus, who comes to live His life through you (John 1:14, 16). In Jesus, you have received "grace upon grace!" Hero, live as a free man, not a slave to sin and Satan. You have been bought off the slave block. Christ has paid the redemption price. *You are free.*

HEAD

- Read Romans 6:1–14 prayerfully. Pay close attention to what Paul is saying.
- Jesus has bought your freedom with His life. You are no longer a slave to the sin life of Adam; you are alive in Christ.

HEART

- What feelings are you experiencing as you read today's entry? Take some time to reflect on what you've read. *Please* do not rush. Write down your feelings and ask God to empower you to work through them.

HANDS

- Type or write in big, bold letters:
      I Am Free! I Have Been Bought Off the Slave Block.
      I Will Know (Romans 6:1–10)
      I Will Reckon (Romans 6:11)
      I Will Surrender (Romans 6:12–14)
      I Am FREE!
- Tape this to your bathroom mirror.
- For the next week, read Romans 6:1–14 twice a day.

TWENTY

HERO, YOU HAVE A FATHER WHO RUNS

But while he was still a long way off, his father saw him and felt compassion, and ran and embraced him and kissed him.

LUKE 15:20 ESV

A FATHER AND HIS TWO SONS (LUKE 15:11–12) | Once upon a time there was a loving father and his two sons. The older son was very religious. The younger son was not. Despite this big difference, they did have something in common. They both were in deep need of grace.

The younger, nonreligious son disgraced his father by saying, "Father, give me the share of the property that is coming to me." Under Jewish law, at the death of their father, the elder son would get two-thirds of the property and the younger one-third (Deuteronomy 21:17). In this culture, a man's standing in the community was based on his land possession. By giving away one-third of his land before his death, not only was the father dishonored by his son's request, but he also would lose his standing in the community.[1] For a son to make this request, he was basically saying, "Hey, old man, I wish you would go ahead and die already." Think of the pain and shame the father experienced.

Surprisingly, the loving father gave his son the property he was to inherit. According to Middle Eastern tradition of that day, the father had every right to kick his son out of the house without giving him anything![2] It seems to me that the father should have smacked his son upside the head and said, "Boy, is ya crazy?" But the father didn't do either one. He also didn't force his son to stay. Why not? Because love and grace never force. They invite.

WHAT HAPPENS IN VEGAS STAYS IN VEGAS (LUKE 15:13–16) | The boy sold the property, got a ton of money, and went to the Las Vegas of his day, the far country where the Gentiles, or non-Jews who did not believe in the one true God, lived. The far country is also symbolic of a fractured relationship with God. The son deserted his father. And for what? Reckless living that covered him in shame and guilt. His trip to Vegas just about killed him.

The Vegas of his day was too fast for him. The women were too wild, and the partying was too much. The boy had gotten in way over his head. His dream life in Vegas turned out to be a nightmare.

In this nightmare that was now his reality, he found himself working for a Gentile. Some religious Jews considered Gentiles lower than dogs. And if working for one was not bad enough, his job was to work with pigs! A Jew working for a Gentile and feeding pigs was as low as he could get. He not only hit bottom, he smashed through the floor. He was spiritually bankrupt.

FROM NONRELIGIOUS TO RELIGIOUS (LUKE 15:17–19) | In the midst of extreme spiritual and physical bankruptcy, he "came to himself." The boy realized his sin and that he needed to go back home and be with his father. Take note of what the boy does next. He rehearses a speech that he will give his father:

> "Father, I have sinned against heaven and before you. I am no longer worthy to be called your son. Treat me as one of your hired servants" (Luke 15:18–19).

First, he thinks that he is no longer worthy to be his father's son, so he will become a hired servant. This is important because an ordinary servant was in some sense a member of the family, but the hired servant, as the son wanted to be, could be fired at a day's notice.

Second, he is a picture of what a nonreligious person looks like who is trying to be religious so as to be accepted by God. Why do I say he tried to be religious? Because he thought that if he became a *hired servant,* his father would receive him back.

Consider this: Religion is always based on serving God to get in good with God. Religion is man's attempt to please God through certain behaviors.

Religion is man saying, "God, look at what I am doing. Is it good enough? Do you accept me now?" A religionist thinks that if he can just behave well enough, God will accept and bless him. This is exactly what the younger son was doing.

I remember when I went from nonreligious to religious. I started speaking at high schools to warn students about the dangers of drugs. I started donating money to worthy causes. My wife and I gave over twenty-five scholarships to at-risk youth to go to college. In 1994, while playing for the Indianapolis Colts, I won the *RCA Man of the Year Award* for community service. Mayor Stephen Goldsmith of Indianapolis even named October 14, 1996, "Derwin Gray Day" for outstanding community service.

Externally, my religious activities looked good, but on the inside, my soul was constantly asking God, "Is this good enough to make up for my past sins? Are you pleased with me now?"

Never forget: The Great Hero cannot be reached through the religion of man. He reaches out to us in grace so we can know Him face-to-face. And it is this intimate grace encounter with Him that leads to a "Jesus way of life" in Jesus' community called the Church.

The younger son wanted to pay for his sins—this is religion. In the "Jesus way of life," Jesus pays the price for your sins—this is grace. Moreover, He gives you His life so you have the power to be the hero He has created you to be. This is grace on top of grace (John 1:16).

Following Jesus is not a religion. It's about a God who reaches out to you in grace, just as you are, so you can become like someone you never thought you could be: His forgiven and deeply loved son.

THE RUNNING FATHER (LUKE 15:20–24) | In the next scene of the story, the father sees his son while he was still a long way off. This means that he has been *looking* and *waiting* for his son to return home. The text speaks of the father's "prodigal," or extravagant, love when it says,

> But while he was still a long way off, his father saw him and felt compassion,
> and ran and embraced him and kissed him (Luke 15:20 esv).

I wonder if the son flinched, thinking his father was going to strike him, when his father embraced and kissed him instead? Instead of blows to the face, he was greeted with kisses to his face. Can you imagine how he must have felt when he realized that he should have been beaten but instead was embraced with grace?

Let's take a closer look at the father, who, by the way, is the star of this story.

First, the looking and waiting father felt compassion for His son. Did you know that God looks with eyes of compassion and waits for you to return home? Even while you are in a far-off country living recklessly? Maybe your far-off country is sexual addiction. Perhaps it is being a workaholic. Is it lying to protect yourself when you blow it? Women, maybe your far country is an eating disorder or an emotional affair.

Second, the father ran to his son. This is very unusual behavior for a distinguished Middle Eastern father.[3] Men of his stature did not run in this culture. So why did he run? It is quite possible that he ran to protect his son. According to a Jewish custom, when a son disgraces and brings shame on his father through sinful behavior, the elders of the city would have intercepted the younger son before he reached his father. They would have taken him to the village center and smashed a pot at his feet, symbolizing his shame and disgrace. This was a legal act of banishment.[4] Then the elders would have told him leave and never return because of his sinful behavior. How extravagant is the father's love for his son to prevent this from happening.

Third, the father put a robe on him, a ring on his hand, shoes on his feet, and prepared meat for a feast. The robe stands for honor. The son dishonored the father, yet the father honors the son. That's grace.

The ring meant the father's authority belonged to the son. The son disrespected his father's authority, yet the father gives it back to him as a gift. That's grace.

The shoes meant that the younger son was his son, not a servant![5] The son wanted to be a hired servant, but the father said, no, you will always be my son. That's grace.

Preparing the fattened calf for a feast meant that it was time to celebrate!

Despite the sin, the disrespect, and the shame, the loving father celebrates his son's return. That's grace.

And it is grace that unleashes God's power and completely changes a person's life!

Perhaps you are asking, "Where's this brat's punishment, D. Gray?" His punishment took place in the far-off country.

Did you know that all of heaven celebrates when a lost, dead son returns home to his Father's love (Luke 15:7, 10)?

I find it interesting that the father totally ignored his son's rehearsed speech and desire to be a hired servant. As Jesus tells this story, He is showing us that access to God is not found through religion, but through His grace.

But the story is not over. Next, we look into the heart of the older religious brother.

THE ANGRY OLDER BROTHER (LUKE 15:25–32) | Beware of religion.

We find the older, religious brother angry that his father would celebrate the return of his younger brother. The older brother was a model of *external* obedience. He faithfully "served" his father for years. Listen to his words:

> I never disobeyed your command, yet you never gave me a young goat
> that I might celebrate with my friends. But when this son of yours
> came, who devoured your property with prostitutes, you killed the
> fattened calf for him (Luke 15:29–30 ESV).

Like a true religionist, he boasts before God! A religionist thinks he is doing God a favor by serving Him and that God owes him.

The recipient of grace boasts only in the work of Jesus (Ephesians 2:8–9; Galatians 6:14).

Religionists, like the older brother, are high on doctrine but low on love. The Great Hero desires His people to be high on both.

Here's a soul-tattoo: *Even though the older brother was religious, he was just as spiritually dead as the younger brother*. He may have appeared on the outside to be the better son to the father, but he was just as dead on the inside. The older brother was also ticked because his younger brother would now re-inherit another third of the property. This cut into the older brother's inheritance.

As the story continues, we find the older son standing outside the house during the homecoming celebration. Think about this: *He refused to go in the house and celebrate his brother's return.* Are you kidding me? His brother was a wreck, slopping around with pigs…now he was home. Before I start throwing stones at the older brother, though, the Great Hero is reminding me how often I, too, act as the older brother. The older brother totally missed the way of Jesus, and so do you and I at times. Do you see yourself as both of these brothers during different seasons of your life?

The older brother had no experience with God's grace, so he could not give grace to his brother. He only experienced empty religion, not a face-to-face love relationship with God.

The father tells his older son "all that I have is yours." Because the older brother did not serve his father out of love, he couldn't understand why his father was treating his brother with such extravagant love.

When I see that this story is about the heart of the Father, I can take my eyes off myself, look to the Great Hero, and learn to love like Him. This allows me to help those I love process the actions of others through the extravagant grace of God.

V. Gray

Both sons were in the far country but in different ways.

Both sons abandoned their father's love in different ways.

The older brother was a religionist and the younger brother was nonreligious. Both were lost. Both tried to *save* themselves, but only one let the Father save him. Only one received grace.

Don't you find it ironic that the son who went to Vegas, chased hookers, and partied like a drunken frat boy was the one who experienced grace and was welcomed into the father's house (which is a picture of our relationship with God)? And that the older religious brother exiles himself outside the house away from the music and dancing?

THE HERO OF THE STORY | The great hero of this story is the father. Often this tale is called the story of the prodigal son. The word *prodigal* means "recklessly extravagant." The story should be called the "Recklessly Extravagant Loving Father." He's the hero of the story, a picture of the Great Hero. And this is the kind of heart that God is trying to form in you and me. Let Him do it so that you can be a recklessly extravagant loving man. It is recklessly extravagant love that changes the world. People who love in this way are the heroes.

HEAD

- Read Luke 15:11–32 twice in one setting. Read slowly and prayerfully.
- God is the Recklessly Extravagant Loving Father.
- Embrace this love, so you can love this way.
- Read Galatians 6:14.

HEART

- What feelings are being stirred in you as you read today's entry? Can you see how God is the star of the story? Can you see yourself as both brothers during different seasons of your life? Write down your feelings and ask God the Holy Spirit to help you embrace the Jesus-forming work He wants to do in your life.

HANDS

- Seek out a way to extend grace to someone you know this week. Practice being an extravagantly loving person.

TWENTY-ONE

HERO, YOU ARE A BRANCH

I am the vine; you are the branches. Whoever abides in me and I in him,
he it is that bears much fruit, for apart from me you can do nothing.

JOHN 15:5 ESV

THE MIND IS WILLING | My mind often persuades me to attempt things I could do in my past when I was a world-class athlete. For example, several years ago, I was preaching in Texas at a Fellowship of Christian Athletes (FCA) Conference. College athletes from all over the state were in attendance. During "free time," many of the football players began playing basketball. Being the competitive guy that I am, I joined them on the court.

My first mistake was in thinking that I could just run on the court without stretching and grab the rim with two hands to do a pull-up like I used to do "back in the day." Yours truly sprinted to the court like a wounded rhino. I jumped. I did not go very high. Then, as gravity called me back to earth, I almost fell down like a drunk man.

My second mistake happened when I took my shirt off like the nineteen-year-old college football players, who didn't have an ounce of body fat. I quickly put it back on when I remembered that my once ripped eight-pack had gone on a long vacation and showed no signs of ever returning.

THE GAME | If my first two mistakes were not enough, the third certainly was. I decided to join three guys on the FCA staff to play against four college students. Those kids beat us like we stole something the first game. The score was humiliating: 15 to 3. My competitive nature could not accept this defeat, so I rallied the men. We were now ready to conquer our opponents.

The next game they beat us 15 to 4.

HUMBLED | The person I was guarding was scoring on me at will. The whole team was lighting me up like a Christmas tree. I couldn't stop them. Here's the deal: We were blown out by three girls and one guy. And the nickname for one of the girls was "Too Tall" because she was 4' 8"! My daughter at that time was 4' 7"! Are you kidding me? My excuse: The girl I was guarding was 6' 2". She set the three-point record at Baylor University to catapult her team to win the Women's NCAA Division I National Championship the next season. I don't know what the other guys' excuses were…but that was mine!

BASKETBALL AND DERWIN, NOT A GOOD IDEA | What if Michael Jordan, arguably the greatest basketball player of all time, had been at this conference and had seen me playing basketball? And what if he walked up to me and said, "D. Gray, I have watched you play. You are not good. You can't shoot. You can't dribble. And your overall basketball IQ is 10 on a scale of 200. But I do have some good news for you. I have a special machine called "The Regenerator" that will allow me to enter your body and play basketball through you. Would you let me do that? All you have to do is allow me to use your mind and body. I will be like a hand, and your body will be the glove. Trust me."

Of course I would allow Michael Jordan to use "The Regenerator" to play basketball through me! Who wouldn't want to play basketball like Mike? Through the empowerment of his machine, all of a sudden I would begin to shoot the ball like Mike. Jump and slam-dunk like Mike. Dribble like Mike. Have the basketball IQ of Mike. I would even began to walk and talk like Mike. Why? Because Michael Jordan would be playing the game of basketball in and through me. My job would be to simply allow him to do what he does best—play basketball.

Tattoo this truth into your soul: *Someone greater than Michael Jordan desires to play the game of life through you…He is the Life!* (John 1:3–4). Just as Michael Jordan is the greatest basketball player of all-time, Jesus lived the greatest life of all-time, and now He wants to live His great life through you. The process by which you do this is by *practicing the discipline of abiding in Him*. I call it a discipline. In our age of distraction it will not be easy.

ABIDING IN CHRIST | In John 15:1–8, Jesus teaches His disciples, and us, a life-transforming truth. He teaches us how to abide in Him. To abide in Him means to remain in Him. The word *abide* expresses dependence and drawing life from a source greater than ourselves. To abide in Christ conveys an attitude of depending and focusing on Jesus, the One who loves you and the One who now lives within you to produce a life of heroic qualities.

————

As I learn to abide, Jesus shows me what is important. Maybe some tasks can wait or don't need to be completed. I need to remember that people are more important than tasks. Oh Lord, live in me like a hand moves a glove!

————

V. Gray

Jesus makes the bold claim: If you abide in me, you *will* produce much fruit (John 15:5). Producing much fruit simply means that your life, over time, will become more spiritually healthy, like His is. It means that the fruit of the Spirit will be evident in your life (Galatians 5:22–23). Fruit is a source of nourishment to your soul and to those in your sphere of influence. When you abide in Jesus, you will have the capacity to nourish nutrient-deficient souls with the fruit of the Spirit. Marinate in that for a moment.

How would your life be different if you could continually abide in Christ in every facet of your life?

EMPTY RELIGION | Jesus also says that if you do not abide in Him, you will not produce fruit (John 15:5). This means that when you do not abide in Jesus, you are living independent of Him. His life and power will not influence yours. You may get good at doing religious stuff, but your soul and your efforts will be fruitless and empty.

THROWN INTO THE FIRE | What in the world does Jesus mean when he says, "If anyone does not abide in me he is thrown away like a branch and withers; and the branches are gathered, thrown into the fire, and burned" (John 15:6 ESV)? In this context, Jesus is not talking about going to hell. A person who is in Christ cannot be taken out of Christ (John 10:28). When we choose not to abide in Jesus, self-centeredness overwhelms us, and the devil influences our thoughts and actions. When you do not abide, you suffer the consequences of your Christless actions.

Case in point, a man that I was mentoring called me, crying, from his 5,000-square-foot empty house. He had chosen to cheat on his wife. I warned him of the consequences of not abiding in Christ. He was thrown into the fire. Through many months of praying, pain, and tough conversation, he and his wife reconciled. My friend and his family experienced this pain because of him choosing not to abide in Christ.

THE ONE PRAYER GOD WILL ANSWER | If you ask the Great Hero to bless and empower you to abide in Christ, He will honor this prayer because it brings Him glory (John 15:8)! This is the one prayer that God will answer with a "yes" every time! God does not and will not honor selfish, self-promoting prayers.

BACK TO LOVE... AGAIN | I love my wife. I love spending time with her. We go golfing together. We go to movies together. We make decisions together...on everything. My wife, besides the Great Hero, is my best friend, by a long shot. I love to hang out and abide with her. Why? Because I love her! I have experienced her deep sacrificial love for me. I spend time with her because I love her. Here's the deal: The more you love Jesus, the more you will depend and focus on Him. This will lead to loving Him and others more. Hero-in-the-making, abide deeply in Jesus and draw life from Him so you can live a heroic life, doing good to those in your sphere of influence.

HEAD

❧ Read John 15:1–11, slowly and prayerfully.
❧ If you practice the discipline of abiding, you will produce fruit. If you do not, you will not produce fruit and you will experience fire.

HEART

❧ What feelings are you experiencing as you read today's entry? Make a list of what prevents you from practicing the discipline of abiding. Write down your feelings and ask God to empower you to work through them.

HANDS

❧ Ask God the Holy Spirit to empower you to practice the discipline of abiding.
❧ Go to a fruit tree farm or visit a home with an apple tree or orange tree. Talk to the farmer or owner about how the tree produces fruit. What does it need to be fruitful?

TWENTY-TWO

HERO, YOU ARE A DISCIPLE

And Jesus came and said to them, "All authority in heaven and on earth has been given to me. Go therefore and make disciples of all nations, baptizing them in the name of the Father and of the Son and of the Holy Spirit, teaching them to observe all that I have commanded you. And behold, I am with you always, to the end of the age."

MATTHEW 28:18–20 ESV

DISCIPLE OR CHRISTIAN | The word *disciple* is used 269 times in the New Testament. The word *Christian*, which was used to mock Jesus' early followers, is used only three times. The word *disciple* means to be a student of a master teacher. And the goal of the disciple is to become like the teacher.

> A disciple is not above his teacher, but everyone when he is fully trained will be like his teacher (Luke 6:40 ESV).

In Jesus' day, young men would carefully choose which rabbi (teacher) they would follow. This decision defined the rest of their lives. When Jesus asked each of the Jewish young men to follow Him, they knew the profound effect it would have on their lives. In essence, Jesus was inviting them to become like Him. He was inviting these young men to ingest His teaching, assume a new identity, join a new community, and live His mission of loving and rescuing the world (John 3:16–17). This often meant leaving everything.

COVERED IN THE "DUST OF THE RABBI" | A rabbi named Yose Ben Yoezer[1] told His disciples to "cover yourself in the dust of your rabbi's feet." The living picture of being covered in the dust of your rabbi came from something everybody saw in Jesus' day. A rabbi would come to town and right behind him would be a group of disciples doing their best to keep up with their rabbi as he went about teaching from place to place. By the end of the day, from walking behind their rabbi, his disciples were covered with dirt from the dust that came from his feet. This was a good thing. It meant they watched how he lived and listened to how he taught so that they could one day live and teach like him.

If I spend my time learning from the people of the world and our culture, then I will reflect them. If my "bible" is a fashion magazine or a talk show, then that is what I will reflect. If the authority in my life is God's Word and I abide in Him, I will reflect Him.

V. Gray

THE COST OF NON-DISCIPLESHIP | Today, hero-in-the-making, Jesus is calling you by name! He's saying, "Follow me. I want to shape your life into a heroic one like mine." From what we learned in our last entry, as you abide in Jesus, His continual indwelling life and the Holy Spirit become the sources of empowerment for you to progressively become like Him.

The cost of non-discipleship is high. When you fail to be covered in the dust of the rabbi, the world is harmed because your unique expression of grace is missing. Marinate in the thought of this: God has graced you with a unique imprint to make an impact on the world. Imagine a world without William Wilberforce or Dr. Martin Luther King Jr. Your growth as a disciple impacts not just you but also those you influence.

The Church, which is not a building or an organization but people who have embraced Jesus' life and the call to follow Him, is hurt also. Consider this: What if a man named Alan Bacon did not grow as a disciple or invest in the life of a young Christ-follower named Derwin Gray in 1997? I vividly remember being on crutches at a small inner-city church listening to Alan teach a Bible study on the book of Acts. I can still hear the patience in his voice as he answered the questions I had. I say Alan had patience because I would call him at all hours of the night. I can still picture how he would love his wife and parent his children with wisdom. I pray that you have an Alan in your life.

This book and the last ten years that I have been in ministry would not be a reality without Alan. If you do not think your discipleship is important to the Church, read this letter I received last year:

> Hi. I wanted to let you know that you really affected me this weekend. I have been through some terrible, troubling things in my life, and I used to resolve to self-mutilation and other harmful things. You are the only person I have ever heard preach that can capture the attention of everyone in the room, no matter the age. When you asked for girls who have been through tough times to come to the front of the room, I literally felt the Holy Spirit inside of me, and I liked it. I just wanted to let you know that you affected a bunch of people that night.

In his commitment to mature as a Christ-follower, Alan Bacon invested in my discipleship which, in turn, empowered me to impact others.

And finally, there is a high personal cost for you if you walk away from discipleship; *you* are hurt because you are missing out on the abundant and heroic life you were created to live (John 10:10). You were created be like Jesus (Romans 8:29). This is a lifelong process called *spiritual formation*. Do not miss out on abundant life. The opposite, the unheroic life, will not only negatively impact you...others will be negatively impacted also.

Disciples of Jesus, it is time to be heroes. All that we need for life and right living is given to us through Christ (2 Peter 1:3). It's time to unleash it!

HEAD

❧   Friends, you are called to join Jesus in making disciples. Read Matthew 28:18–20 and Luke 6:40.

HEART

❧   What feelings are being called out in you as you read today's entry? Begin to see yourself as Jesus' student, following Him as He lives and teaches. Envision yourself walking behind Him on the dusty roads of Palestine and being covered in His dust. Write about your feelings and ask God to empower you to work through them.

HANDS

❧   If you do not have an Alan-type mentor in your life, ask God to bring wise, faithful Christ-followers to disciple you in the faith. And ask God to also bring someone into your life for you to disciple.

TWENTY-THREE

HERO, YOU ARE GOD'S ATHLETE, PART I

You've all been to the stadium and seen the athletes race. Everyone runs; one wins.
Run to win. All good athletes train hard. They do it for a gold medal that tarnishes
and fades. You're after one that's gold eternally. I don't know about you, but I'm
running hard for the finish line. I'm giving it everything I've got. No sloppy living
for me! I'm staying alert and in top condition. I'm not going to get caught napping,
telling everyone else all about it and then missing out myself.

1 CORINTHIANS 9:24–27 THE MESSAGE

THE PRIZE | On October 30, 1986, I wrote my life's mission on a piece
of paper. I taped it to the wall right above my bedroom door. It was a short
mission statement that captured my imagination and shaped my life. Even this
morning as I write this book, pray for my children, and get ready to celebrate
Valentine's Day with my queen and bride, it still stirs my soul.

I want to be the best ever.

Those seven words were all I wrote. Every morning, this mission
statement stared at me. It called me to action. It challenged me. It inspired
me through distractions, distress, and disappointment. Throughout the day at
school my mission statement whispered to me, "What are you doing to make
me a reality?" At night before I closed my eyes to sleep, there it was hanging
above my door, whispering, "Did you take the difficult path to make me live?"

I did not become the best football player ever. I haven't tackled anyone in
an NFL game in eleven years. There was no big celebration when I retired. My
point is this: I did not become the best football player ever to grace the NFL,

but I do think I became the best football player *I could be.* Here's the deal: *Hunger to be all that God has made you to be!* For many of you disciples of Jesus, you are not hungry enough for the heroic life that awaits you. Stop aiming low! It's time to aim high. Living life on mission with Jesus is as high as it gets.

THE REAL MISSION: THE TWO "GREATS" | Hero-in-the-making, you are a disciple of the Master Teacher, Jesus. You are His student in the school of *the eternal kind of life.* He has written a mission statement for your life:

> And Jesus came and said to them, "All authority in heaven and on earth has been given to me. Go therefore and make disciples of all nations, baptizing them in the name of the Father and of the Son and of the Holy Spirit, teaching them to observe all that I have commanded you. And behold, I am with you always, to the end of the age" (Matthew 28:18–20 ESV).

As a disciple, your mission is to celebrate, champion, and copartner with the Father, the Son, and the Holy Spirit in His plan of rescuing this broken planet that He unceasingly and extravagantly loves. Whether you are a doctor, a truck driver, or a schoolteacher, this is your mission. You have been placed where you are by the Great Hero to be His missionary.

The *Great Commission* is accomplished through *the Great Commandment:*

> "Which commandment is the most important of all?" Jesus answered, "The most important is, 'Hear, O Israel: The Lord our God, the Lord is one. And you shall love the Lord your God with all your heart and with all your soul and with all your mind and with all your strength.' The second is this: 'You shall love your neighbor as yourself.' There is no other commandment greater than these" (Mark 12:28–31 ESV).

The mission is accomplished by loving God, yourself, and your neighbor, wherever you find yourself. As you live a dynamic, Jesus-centered life, the outflow is loving people. And it is in and through the Jesus-life indwelling in you that others are invited to embrace Him. Like an athlete, you must train.

Just as I trained to become a fine-tuned football player, you must train to become a fine-tuned disciple. This beautiful, life-giving, heroic life is a daily walk of dependence and discipline. The road that you walk on will be filled with disappointment, celebration, and pain.

Life is simplified when I embrace my life's mission. Keeping this focus enables me to filter life's decisions through my mission statement—much like that of a company. Thank You, Lord, that You live in me and through me to accomplish this.

V. Gray

DEPENDENCE AND DISCIPLINE | For many of us, we slide into two extremes regarding our spiritual training. One option is, we may overemphasize our role and minimize God. The person who does this tries to live *for Jesus*. But, Jesus is God. He is ETERNAL LIFE! He does not need us to live for Him (Acts 17:25)! We need Him to live in, through, and *for us* (Ephesians 2:1–5). This person lives by rules, rededication efforts, and busyness for Jesus. This is unheroic.

The other option is the opposite extreme: we overemphasize God's role and minimize our role. This person is spiritually passive. He focuses on a once-a-week experience at a Sunday worship service. He thinks God will nuke his sin problems and fix all his issues with a push of a button. He does not have a disciplined spiritual training plan to grow as a disciple. He is like the guy who says he wants to drop thirty pounds, but he doesn't eat healthy food or exercise. This extreme is also unheroic.

The balance that the Great Hero is looking for is found in Philippians 2:12–13:

> Therefore, my beloved, as you have always obeyed, so now, not only as in my presence but much more in my absence, work out your own salvation with fear and trembling, for it is God who works in you, both to will and to work for his good pleasure (ESV).

In this text, we see the perfect balance of dependence and discipline. We are to be disciplined and work out salvation with fear or respect for God because it is God who works in us. So here's the deal: *Without God, we cannot grow spiritually as disciples—and without our willingness, God will not grow us as disciples.*

Hero-in-the making, are you, in and through Jesus, living in dependence on the Holy Spirit and disciplining yourself to be His disciple?

Do not be satisfied with just being a Sunday morning spectator! It's time for our generation to wake up to the ancient call of joining God on His mission by relentlessly and passionately loving God, ourselves, and our neighbors. Let us, through dependence and discipline, love so Christlike that our love commands and demands explanation.

This is our mission. Does it capture your imagination?

HEAD

- Read your life's mission statement in Matthew 28:18–20.
- Read Mark 12:28–31. This is how you, along with all of Jesus' disciples, are to fulfill this mission.
- You are God's athlete. You are His disciple. You are a hero.

HEART

- What feelings are being stirred in you as you read today's entry? How did you feel about the Great Commission being your mission statement? How do you feel about your mission being fulfilled through Jesus and the Great Commandment? Write down your feelings and ask God to empower you to work through them. Be honest and wrestle with God.

HANDS

- Write or type out the Great Commission and the Great Commandment. Then place them above your door. In the same way, place your mission statement somewhere where it will look at you.
- As you go to school, work, the gym, or out to eat, you are on mission. All of life is Jesus' mission. Talk to someone about this entry.

TWENTY-FOUR

HERO, YOU ARE GOD'S ATHLETE, PART II

Train yourself for godliness; for while bodily training is of some value, godliness is of value in every way, as it holds promise for the present life and also for the life to come.

1 TIMOTHY 4:7–8 ESV

THE AGE OF DISTRACTION | What captures your imagination and inspires you to action? Is it the Great Hero and His mission? Or is it your favorite reality show, Blackberry, iPhone, movies, video games, sports, romance novels, business, current events, or the Internet?

> *Someone or something*
>> *is going to capture your imagination,*
>>> *and it will move you to some sort of action.*

As God's athletes, living a *dependent* and *disciplined* life will enable you to focus on the Great Hero and His Great Mission. Several years ago God taught me a lesson about depending on Him. I was golfing, something I'm not very good at but still enjoy. I was about 155 yards from the green when I confidently grabbed my 7-iron and swung it at the ball like Barry Bonds going for a home run. My logic was simple: Swing hard and the ball will go far and land on the green. I swung hard, and the ball sliced into the woods, killing a bird. Just kidding...but if it would have hit a bird, the bird would have died.

Out of frustration, I did the exact same thing again and got the exact same results. Before I swung again, I grabbed my club and preached to it like a TV evangelist, "Hey, 7-iron, you are designed to go a 155 yards, and I am going to swing easy and allow you to do your job." Next thing I knew

I hit a high, beautiful shot that landed softly on the green. In the midst of my celebration and Michael Jackson dancing impersonation, I sensed God say, "The same way you let the 7-iron do its job, let me do my job in and through you."

That simple spiritual lesson on the golf course shaped my spirituality as much as completing my Master of Divinity degree! It will transform yours, as well. Let the Great Hero do His job in and through you.

SPIRITUAL EXERCISE | When it comes to spiritual exercise, I realize that *dependence on Jesus actually empowers us to live a life of incorporating spiritual disciplines* (1 Corinthians 15:10).

Prayer. Prayer is not approaching God with a wish list, like a five-year-old leaves for Santa on the kitchen table on Christmas Eve. God already knows what you need (Matthew 6:32). Prayer is face-to-face intimacy with our King and Papa. It is a conversation with the Greatest Being who is, who was, and who always will be. Prayer is a meeting place where dialogue between two friends occurs. Prayer is where we release our fears and burdens, ask questions and learn to listen, and become challenged by God. Prayer is not just a scheduled one-time appointment during our "quiet time." It is an ongoing, abiding dialogue with God as we *practice His presence in all of life's activities.* In the next entry, I will explore the gift of prayer.

Feasting on the Word of God. As a football player, I knew that if I studied my playbook, I could play better in the games because I would know what I was doing. When I became one of God's athletes, I realized that God gave His players a playbook called the Bible. So I committed to read it and embrace its teaching (Ezra 7:10). Soon, I realized that the more I read the sacred Book, the more God fed my soul with Himself. I experienced why He is called the Bread of Life (John 6:35). Feasting on the Word of God is more than downloading information. Feasting transforms lives (John 5:39–40).

So how can you read the Bible in a way that leads to transformation? I want to introduce you to an ancient discipline called *lectio divina.* This Latin word simply means "sacred reading." In the book *Life With God,* authors Richard Foster and Kathryn A. Helmers explain this study method using these six points[1]:

Lectio divina means that as you feast on the Word of God, it is essential that you *slow down and listen* as you read the text of scripture. You sit at God's feet and listen…not rushing like a channel-flipper looking for another show.

It means that you *surrender* to the text of scripture you are reading. You allow its message to master you, instead of you mastering it. You allow God's soul food to penetrate the deep parts of your being.

It means that you *marinate* in the text you are engaging. You allow your mind, will, and emotions, through the Spirit's encouragement, to become fully engaged in God's story that is being revealed.

It means that you *pray* during the reading of the scripture. You allow the magnitude of God's story and His passion for this broken planet to become your story and passion. You may find yourself praying for coworkers, confessing, or just crying in gratitude for what Jesus has done for humanity.

It means that you *apply* the text of scripture to your life. You will be encouraged, amazed, and challenged as the Great Hero allows life's circumstances to force you to live what you are reading. The Spirit will deposit truth in you, so you can live out that truth in the context of everydayness.

Finally, it means *obeying* the text of scripture. The call of a disciple is to obey Jesus (Matthew 28:18–20). And the Master Teacher will never command you to do anything that He does not provide you with the power to get the job done.

Remember, you are still trying to understand the author's original intent and the context in which he is writing. I encourage you to not just have a Bible study where you collect biblical facts. May the reading of your Bible be like sitting at your favorite coffee shop across the table from a close friend who loves you and connects with you as you learn the ways of life from Him.

All of life is worship. As Jesus' student on mission with Him, all of life is sacred! The only thing that you can do that is not sacred is sin (1 Corinthians 10:31). When you go to work, school, the movies, or on a date, you carry the Father, the Son, and the Holy Spirit with you. All of life is sacred ground because the sacred God lives in you. It is a discipline to remember this beautiful reality. As you practice this discipline, watch how you begin to see all of life differently. Even the most mundane things become a sacred adventure.

Solitude and silence. We live in a loud, distracting world. It is vital that you take time to get away from the noise and unplug. This is called the discipline of solitude and silence. Solitude simply means finding a quiet place and time, away from our phones, TVs, and other people, just to be with God in complete silence. If you do not take time to occasionally pull away from distractions and people, distractions and people will pull you away from the Great Hero and His Great Mission.

———

Why would I expect to be fruitful for Christ if I have allowed things of the world to pull me away from Him and His Great Mission? To know this is actually an encouragement. God has great works He desires to do through me— I want to be a part of that!

V. Gray

———

Community. You need people and people need you. When you embraced Jesus, He brought you into His kingdom as an individual for the purpose of grafting you into His family of disciples. You are a first-round draft pick on the Ultimate Team. You need people in your life who will encourage you— and you need people in your life to encourage.

Lions, when hunting, always look for prey that is not protected by a herd. There is a roaring lion looking to devour disciples who are not protected within a community (1 Peter 5:8). Hero-in-the-making, it is a discipline to be involved in a community. It is also a gift to have a community…even though a community can be messy.

Fasting. Fasting is the spiritual exercise of not eating for a certain period of time. You deprive yourself of physical nourishment for the purpose of spiritual sustenance. *Fasting increases your focus on the Great Hero.* It will also develop your ability for self-denial and self-control. I fast one day a week from sunup to sundown and when I feel a hunger pain, I pray for the needs of others. The Spirit will guide you into how He wants you to fast. You may want to fast from TV, coffee, or sex with your spouse. Be creative.

ONE SIZE DOES NOT FIT ALL | I did not tell you how to do these spiritual exercises or how often to do them for a reason. One size does not fit all when it comes to spiritual exercises. Get on your face and pray. The Holy Spirit will teach you over time how to implement these exercises in your own life.

Disciple, the mission is before us. Our world is filled with broken people in need of the living grace that is in you. It is time to get in shape for the task.

Train often.

Train hard.

And most importantly, train in the Spirit's power, through the indwelling life of Jesus.

HEAD

- Reread 1 Timothy 4:7–8 by using the *lectio divina* discipline.
- In our age of distractions, spiritual exercises will sharpen your focus on Jesus and His mission.

HEART

- What feelings are you experiencing as you read today's entry? How were you encouraged by this entry? How were you challenged by it? Why do you think you are more comfortable in distraction than in silence? Write down your feelings and ask God to empower you to work through them.

HANDS

- Get in shape! Train hard. Train often. And most importantly, train in the Spirit's power, through the indwelling life of Jesus.
- If you feel led by the Holy Spirit, consider fasting for one meal or one day this month.
- Ask a trusted friend about how he or she practices spiritual exercises in his or her own life.

TWENTY-FIVE

HERO, JESUS TEACHES YOU HOW TO PRAY

Pray like this…

MATTHEW 6:9 NLT

THE GIFT OF PRAYER | Prayer is a gift. But for many, prayer causes frustration and confusion. You are frustrated because you think you do not pray enough, right? You are confused because you really do not know how to pray, and it seems like when you do pray, your prayers hit the ceiling anyway.

Don't feel bad. Prayer frustrated and confused Jesus' first followers, as well. To help His disciples and you learn to cultivate a lifestyle of prayer, Jesus gave us a pattern to embrace and make our own in Matthew 6:9–13:

> Pray then like this: "Our Father in heaven, hallowed be your name. Your kingdom come, your will be done, on earth as it is in heaven. Give us this day our daily bread, and forgive us our debts, as we also have forgiven our debtors. And lead us not into temptation, but deliver us from evil (ESV).

This has been called the Lord's Prayer. I like to call it the *Disciples' Prayer*. In this guide to prayer, He didn't mean for us to rehearse it word for word like something that is lifeless. This is the living God teaching His living people to live a lifestyle of prayer. The Disciples' Prayer is a gift to guide you as you find communion with the Great Hero.

THE DISCIPLES' PRAYER | Here is an example of how I use the Disciples' Prayer as a guide as I prepare to live on mission with Jesus:

Our Father in heaven, hallowed (honored and respected above all) be your name. Papa, thank you that I have the privilege of calling you *Papa.* You are not a cold, distant, angry God. You love me with a love that is face-to-face, life-forming, and real. I join with all of heaven in celebrating your uniqueness, majesty, awesomeness, and kingship. I can only approach Your throne of grace and mercy because of the life, death, and resurrection of your beloved Son, Jesus, and through the power of the Holy Spirit. Thank you for the gift of Your nearness. Thank You that "Your cell phone is always on" and I can reach You. May I treasure and love You above all. And Papa, empower me to live in such a way that others will treasure and love You above all, too.

Your kingdom come, Your will be done, on earth as it is in heaven. Papa, You love this broken planet so much that You gave Jesus for every single person that has ever lived (1 John 2:2). May Your mission and passion to rescue humanity and restore creation unto Yourself be mine (2 Corinthians 5:19, Ephesians 1:9-10). Your kingdom is a kingdom of love, courage, and justice…this is what heaven looks like. You have empowered me and all Your disciples to give glimpses of heaven on earth. May all Your people shine like the stars in heaven glorifying you (Matthew 5:16). May Your kingdom come to my home, my extended family, the church I pastor, the school my children attend, the city I live in, and eventually the world. May Your kingdom and Your will express itself in and through me, all for Your honor.

Give us this day our daily bread. Papa, my daily Bread is Jesus (John 6:35); He is what I need most. May I worship You in all of life. May I abide in You continually. Please empower me to provide for my family and those in need as I work hard with the abilities You have graciously given me. Give me the power to trust You to provide for my *daily needs, and not my daily greeds.* Papa, empower me to love my wife with a sacrificial, soul-beautifying love. May I love and parent Presley and Jeremiah in such a way that they treasure and love You above all. Bless me as a pastor to lead with the courage of Joshua, the determination of Nehemiah, and the single-minded focus of Paul as I serve the people You have entrusted to me. Papa, bless the writing of this book. May it set hearts ablaze with a sacred passion for You and Your mission. You are my daily Bread; constantly feed my soul.

And forgive us our debts, as we also have forgiven our debtors. Papa, I am eternally grateful that all my sin—past, present, and future—has been nailed to the cross of Jesus (Colossians 2:13–15). May the ocean of forgiveness that I swim in forever grip my soul to the point that I forgive those who have wounded me even when I do not want to do so (Ephesians 4:32). I no longer want to be held prisoner by the dark dungeon of unforgiveness.

And lead us not into temptation, but deliver us from the evil one (NIV). Papa, thank you that I belong to You and not the evil one. Thank You that just as Jesus defeated Satan in the wilderness by Your power, so can I (Matthew 4:1–11). Thank You that Jesus defeated the powers of darkness on the cross (Colossians 2:13–15) and for giving me Your full armor to defeat the evil one and advance Your kingdom in every area of my life (Ephesians 6:10–20).

AN EXAMPLE | I have tried to give you a living example of how the Disciples' Prayer guides me. Prayer is vital to your intimacy with the Great Hero, and it is essential to your growth in the eternal kind of life. As you begin to pray this way, *use your own language and thoughts.* Your Papa is concerned with your heart, not your eloquence of speech. And do not go by your feelings as a gauge to determine if you have connected with God. Our face-to-face connection with the Great Hero is not based on our feelings; it is anchored in His commitment to His children.

When I rest in this truth, it takes the pressure off me to "perform." It makes me want to spend more time with my heavenly Papa because the grace He gives means I don't have to. It frees me to just be with Him.

V. Gray

WHY DO PRAYERS GO UNANSWERED? | Why do our prayers go unanswered? I offer six reasons, based on my reading of William Lane Craig's *Hard Questions, Real Answers.*[1]

First, sin in our lives. If you are willfully living in sin, God will not answer our prayers (Psalm 66:18). When I do not sacrificially love my bride, God will not answer my prayer (1 Peter 3:7). And if you are consciously living in sin, your prayers will be selfish.

Second, selfish motives. So often our prayers are selfish (James 4:3). We treat the Great Hero like He is a vending machine; if we press the right button, God is obligated to give us what we desire. I am so thankful God has not answered my selfish prayers. If He would have given me what I asked for, I would have destroyed myself and those around me.

Third, a lack of faith. When we pray in God's will, we can pray with confidence. Sadly, many Christ-followers are double-minded and doubt when they pray (James 1:6–8). God does not answer the prayers of a double-minded man. Now, we must balance this truth with Jesus saying that the faith required for God to do mighty things through our prayers does not have to be great (Luke 17:6). So here's the deal: God answers your prayers because your faith is in Him, not faith in the size of the faith you have.

What about physical healing?[2] Some well meaning Christ-followers mistakenly believe that through the death of Jesus, or His atonement (Isaiah 53:5), Christ-followers should never be sick. If you are sick, just pray with enough faith and you will be healed. Friends, this is simply unbiblical and damaging to the cause of Christ. God can and does heal today—but He is not required to. For example, Paul couldn't heal Timothy's stomach problem (1 Timothy 5:23) nor could he heal Trophimus at Miletus (2 Timothy 4:20) or Epaphroditus (Philippians 2:25–27). Paul spoke of "a bodily illness" he had (Galatians 4:13–15). God allowed Job to go through a terrible season of physical suffering (Job 1–2).

The Bible teaches us that our physical bodies are continuously running down. Our present bodies are perishable, weak, and decaying (1 Corinthians 15:42–44; 2 Corinthians 4:16). Friends, death and disease will be a part of the human condition until we receive resurrection bodies that are immune to death and disease (1 Corinthians 15:51–55). Should we pray for physical healing? Yes! And if God chooses not to heal us, we trust that He is performing a greater work in us then just physical healing.

Fourth, a lack of seriousness. Many of our prayers go unanswered because we do not really care if they get answered. When I prayed for my wife as she battled cancer, my prayers were serious. Others times, my prayers have not been as serious. When you pray, pray with great dependence in God, asking Him to do great things through your prayers. And when someone asks you to pray, do it right there on the spot. If you wait till later, you will not do it.

Fifth, a lack of perseverance. Closely related to our seriousness as we pray is perseverance. Some of our prayers go unanswered because we give up too easily. We pray once or twice and then we stop. Keep on praying (Luke 11:5–13).

Sixth, a lack of not praying in God's will. According to 1 John 5:14–15, if we pray in God's will, He will answer our prayers. So the question is, how do we pray in God's will? A great place to start is by looking again at the Disciples' Prayer and by looking at how the apostle Paul prayed. Read Ephesians 1:17–22, 3:14–21; Philippians 1:9–11; and 2 Thessalonians 1:11–12.

Are these the kind of prayers that you pray? These are the kind of prayers I want to pray. These are the kind of prayers that God's answers.

Without a growing, Christ-centered, Christ-magnifying, and Christ-enthralled prayer life, living a heroic life is an impossibility. Please be patient with yourself! It will take time, like anything in life, to cultivate a lifestyle of prayer. I am praying for your prayer life. Please pray for mine as well.

HEAD

- Patiently and prayerfully reread Matthew 6:9–13; Ephesians 1:17–22, 3:14–21; Philippians 1:9; and 2 Thessalonians 1:11–12.
- Jesus has taught you to pray in the Disciples' Prayer. Use this framework as your sacred guide to face-to-face communion with the Great Hero.

HEART

- What are you feeling as you read today's entry? Is there an aspect of prayer that you avoid or one that you spend a lot of time on? *Please* do not rush. Write down your feelings and ask God to empower you to work through them.

HANDS

- Write the Disciples' Prayer on a note card or in your PDA.

SECTION THREE

THE OUTWARD JOURNEY

TWENTY-SIX

HERO, EMBRACE THE GREAT STORY

As you [Father] sent me [Jesus] into the world,
so I have sent them [all Christ-followers] into the world.

JOHN 17:18 ESV

CAPTIVATED BY GREAT STORIES | As humans, it is hardwired into our spiritual DNA to be fascinated and inspired to action by great stories. My generation was captivated by the story of Rocky Balboa, the Italian Stallion. Balboa was an out-of-luck street brawler working for the Philadelphia mob. He catches a few breaks and lands a fight with Apollo Creed, the heavyweight champion. In the first fight, Apollo escapes with a narrow victory. Even though Rocky loses, you feel like he won — especially at the end of the fight when he cries his love's name, "Adrian!" in the hardly intelligible language of *Rocktonian*. In the next fight, Rocky defeats Creed in the battle of all battles.

This epic story so mesmerized my generation that Sylvester Stallone made fifty-seven more *Rocky* movies!… Just kidding. Stallone *only* made six more *Rocky* movies. I was so moved by the story that I would watch *Rocky III* before football games! I was inspired by his work ethic and "never-quit" attitude that empowered him to victory against superior opponents. If Rocky could do it, so could I!

Great stories capture our imagination. How about *The Chronicles of Narnia: The Lion, the Witch and the Wardrobe?* I was moved to tears and applause when Aslan, the Jesus figure of the story, rose from the dead after dying to save the life of Edmund. I lost it when the resurrected Aslan got to the great battle and roared at the Satan character. When she saw and heard his roar, the wicked White Witch uttered the word, "Impossible!" I imagine that was what Satan said when Jesus kicked open the tomb where His body laid for three days.

I am captivated by these great stories!

What stories capture your imagination?

EMBRACE THE GREAT STORY | The Great Story is not a movie; it's not written in just any book…it is told in the Great Book. The Great Story is also a life lived in God's unfolding drama of rescuing and restoring humanity and planet Earth. If you do not embrace the Great Story, your life will make no sense, Jesus Christ will make no sense, and the Church will make no sense.

Like any great story, it starts with the hero. God is the Hero of the Great Story. As we have learned in earlier entries, the Great Hero is the ultimate expression of glory, power, perfection, and love. He has eternally existed as Father, Son, and Holy Spirit—the tri-personal God. The Great Hero uses His creative genius to bring about a universe that is perfectly and intelligently designed for life to exist on Earth. And on this third rock from the sun, in a peaceful garden, He creates His masterpiece: Adam and Eve.

These image-bearers were created out of the Great Hero's unceasing love so they could love Him, love each other, and care for creation. They were God's first community and representatives. Just as the Great Hero rules heaven, they were to rule the earth. God places the Tree of Life and the Tree of the Knowledge of Good and Evil in the Garden of Eden. The Tree of Life represents a face-to-face, life-giving relationship with God. And the Tree of the Knowledge of Good and Evil represents man living life independent and in rebellion against his Maker. Why would God put these trees in the Garden? Because just as I want my children to *choose* to love me, the Great Hero wants His children to choose to love Him.

But great tragedy enters the peaceful garden when Satan, a beautiful angel, becomes an enemy of God and His image-bearers. He is hell-bent on spreading evil, rebellion, and death. Through his craftiness, he deceives our willing ancestors to doubt God's goodness and eat from the Tree of the Knowledge of Good and Evil: "For God knows that when you eat of it your eyes will be opened, and you will be like God, knowing good and evil" (Genesis 3:5 ESV).

The Great Story now has a great conflict.

***MISSIO DIE*—THE GOD OF MISSION** | The Great Hero is the Great Missionary.

God's mission began with a man named Abraham, and through him the tiny nation of Israel was birthed. Israel was God's chosen people, a kingdom of priests, His prized possession (Exodus 19:1–6). They received God's blessing so that they could be a blessing to the nations that did not know the One True God (Genesis 12:1–3; Deuteronomy 7:7–8, Acts 13:17). The nation of Israel was the Great Hero's missionary.

God set Israel apart from other nations through the way He commanded them to live. He also gave Israel a sacrificial system to follow so their sins could be forgiven. This sacrificial system was only temporary because one day the Messiah (Anointed One), the sinless Lamb of God, would come to earth and die for the sins of the world (Hebrews 9:11–14; John 1:29). In the Old Testament, 191 prophecies foretold of the Jewish Messiah and Savior.[1] Each was literally fulfilled in the life, death, resurrection, and ascension of Jesus of Nazareth.

The Great Hero's mission continues as Jesus, the Jewish Messiah, enters time and space as the world's Savior. He is sent to obliterate sin, Satan, and death! This is why the early church fathers used the Latin words *missio dei* to describe God. *He is the God of mission.* And now, God's mission is continued through the Church. Reflect on Jesus' words:

> As you (Father) sent me (Jesus) into the world, so I have sent them (all Christ-followers) into the world (John 17:18 ESV).

PAUSE | It is vital that you see yourself in light of the Great Hero's Great Story. You are living in this unfolding drama and have an important role to play. You have been created in this time and in your sphere of influence to play a key role in the Great Story.

Refuse to live by little stories anymore. You were designed to live the great adventure of the Great Story. Despite entertainment everywhere in America, we are bored, self-absorbed, and a depressed people. Why? It is because we are spiritually dying while trying to live in our little stories. Your soul was made for the Great Story! Start living it!

———

If anyone should ever question his or her worth, this would be the antidote! We are not only valuable, but we are on a high-stakes mission with the God of the universe! Lord, let this be the energy You provide to empower us to live on mission with You.

V. Gray

———

Marinate your heart and mind in this: Your mission originates in the very nature of our tri-personal God. God the Father sent the Son; the Father and Son sent the Holy Spirit; and now the Father, the Son, and the Holy Spirit send His people, the Church, into the world to be His ambassadors (2 Corinthians 5:18–20). The people of God, His followers, are the physical embodiment of the tri-personal God on earth. That's you and me and all of Jesus' disciples (John 14:23; John 17:8). Wow! The weight of this reality compels me to bow down and pray for courage to embrace this call.

If you embrace this reality, think about how going to work or school will become filled with eternal implications. They will become your sacred vocation.

If you embrace this reality, think about how this impacts your marriage, parenting, or singleness.

If you embrace the Great Story, you will live a heroic life that crashes into eternity, leaving a wake of goodness, courage, and restoration behind.

We are captivated by great stories. May the Great Story of the Great Hero capture your imagination and spur you to action in God's power (Colossians 1:27–28).

It's time to live.

It's time to embrace your mission.

It's time to embrace the hero within you...not just for your good, but for the good of the world (Matthew 5:16).

In the next entry, we'll take a look at the Church and its role in God's rescue mission.

HEAD

* Read John 17:8 and 2 Corinthians 5:18–20.
* If you do not embrace and live the Great Story, your life will make no sense, Jesus will make no sense, and the Church will make no sense.
* Your mission originates in the very nature of our tri-personal God who sends His people, the Church, into the world to be His ambassadors. The physical embodiment of the tri-personal God on earth is the people of God—you and me, and all of Jesus' followers.

HEART

* What feelings are being stirred in you as you read today's entry? How were you encouraged by it? How were you challenged by it? How has it impacted your view of your role on the earth and the Church's role? Write down your feelings and ask God to empower you to work through them.

HANDS

* Develop a plan to read through the Bible. A One-Year Bible or Bible reading plan can help you commit to reading through the Great Story.

TWENTY-SEVEN

HERO, YOU ARE THE *ECCLESIA*

"And I tell you, you are Peter, and on this rock I will build my church, and the gates of hell shall not prevail against it."

MATTHEW 16:18 ESV

CHURCH | God's number one means for changing the world is through His community of people called the *ecclesia*, or Church. The Church is at the *epicenter* of the Great Hero's rescue mission. Let the shock of that statement settle in your soul. As we learned in the previous entry, Jesus believed that His followers would continue His mission. Listen to Him again:

> As you (Father) sent me (Jesus) into the world, so I have sent them (all Christ-followers) into the world (John 17:18 ESV).

Friends, being *the Church* is a big deal. Please do not reduce something as precious and important to God as the Church is to just somewhere you go on Sundays to listen to a guy give a talk.

WHERE DO YOU GO TO CHURCH? | If you would have asked first-century Jesus-followers, "Where do you go to church?" they would have looked at you with strange expressions on their faces. They would not have understood the question, because the word "church" has nothing to do with a building where people go on Sunday for an hour and fifteen minutes (and for some cultures, make that three hours).

The church is Jesus' community of followers. It's His disciples. It is a people, not a place. You, friend, are the Church!

ECCLESIA | Paul, the one-time enemy of Jesus (Galatians 1:23), used the Greek term *ecclesia* to describe a gathering of Jesus' disciples. Many dictionaries will tell you that *ecclesia* literally means "the gathering of the called-out ones."[1] *Ecclesia* comes from two words—*ek*, meaning "out," and *kaleo*, meaning "to call."

Ecclesia wasn't even a religious term; it has more of a political aspect to it. In Paul's time, an ecclesia was a gathering of elders in a community. In smaller villages and towns across Judea, local leaders gathered regularly to discuss and deliberate over a variety of social and political dilemmas facing the community. The ecclesia was a gathering of wise community leaders brought together by their common vision for the harmony and well-being of the community as a whole. In essence, the ecclesia was a community within a community whose function was to add value to the place in which they lived.

As the modern-day ecclesia, we must embrace and see ourselves as *sent* by Jesus into the society of which we are a part, to add value, to bring wisdom, to cultivate a better community (John 17:8). Through abiding in Christ, our lives are an invitation to those not yet in the ecclesia to join us as they see us doing good and blessing our sphere of influence (Matthew 5:16, 28:18–20; 2 Corinthians 5:18–21).

Essentially, the ecclesia is a community of Jesus Christ look-alikes that infiltrate every facet of society, doing good and infecting noncarriers of grace with grace. At the core of God's rescue and healing mission on planet Earth is His community called the Church.

BORN-AGAIN IDENTITY | As the Great Hero's ecclesia, we all have a new identity. 1 Peter 2:9 describes it:

> But you are a chosen race, a royal priesthood, a holy nation, a people
> for his own possession, that you may proclaim the excellencies of him
> who called you out of darkness into his marvelous light (ESV).

Ecclesia, this is who you are. *Hero, you are in the chosen race.* The Middle Eastern understanding of the word *chosen* expresses a mission or task for a community of people to fulfill. Because you follow Jesus, you are a part of His chosen race, which means you are in the new humanity (2 Corinthians 5:17), infused with a new source of life (Galatians 2:20), and living with a new mission (Matthew 28:18–20).

A proper understanding of the word *chosen* assassinates what I call the "selfish gospel," which is not a gospel at all. The selfish gospel goes like this: Jesus died for my sins so I can go to heaven when I die. Is that it? The glorious work of Jesus is boiled down to a simple "get-out-of-hell-free" pass! That is a selfish gospel! It is a gospel that my generation is sick of and rejects! It is unheroic.

King Jesus lived a perfect life on your behalf because you could not.

Glorious Jesus died a bloody, painful, and dehumanizing death on the cross in your place to satisfy God's righteous anger against your sin.

Victorious Jesus rose from the dead so your life can be infused with His *eternal kind of life* and you can be a source of good to the world, unleashing the kingdom of God like He did.

The gospel empowers you to be a blessing to the world.

The gospel is Good News that transforms you to be a hero for the sake of the world. And yes, we receive the *eternal kind of life.* This unending life begins now and continues forever in the new heaven and new earth (Revelation 21:1–4).

As the ecclesia—like Jesus who indwells you—you live to serve the world (Matthew 20:28).

As the ecclesia—you, me, and disciples all over the world—we are insurgents of grace, strategically positioned by God in our spheres of influence.

Royal Priesthood: Everyone that makes up the ecclesia is a royal priest. This does not mean that everyone is a pastor, but it does mean that you can go directly to God yourself. The word *priest* originates from a Latin word that means *bridge*. In essence, you are a bridge that Jesus uses to connect non-Christ-followers to Himself.

How many of us Jesus-people waste our lives by not recognizing that we are God's priests and missionaries? Our minds are charmed by little stories instead of being captivated by the Great Story! *All of life is your priestly pulpit of grace to humanity* starting in your home and then moving out into your spheres of influence. To paraphrase St. Francis of Assisi: Preach it! And when your life demands an explanation…use words.

Knowing that the Good News is so much more than a trip to heaven prepares me to live a life of adventure and purpose. Realizing that I am an "insurgent of grace" in God's army excites me; it reiterates my value and significance and reason for being on this earth.

V. Gray

Holy Nation. The Great Hero is in the sacred work of building a community of people to reflect His kingdom to the world. You are a part of a worldwide community called the *ecclesia.* You are a part of His great nation within the nations.

In Revelation 7:9, we see a beautiful picture of all ethnic groups worshiping Jesus—together. Not segregated. If the worship of Jesus is ethnically diverse in heaven, why is that not the case in 93 percent of Bible-believing churches in the U.S.?[2] Sunday morning sadly remains the most segregated time in America. Shouldn't we begin to practice what we will be doing for all eternity?

Instead of complaining about the racial and socioeconomic segregation in our churches, two other pastors and I decided to start a multiethnic, intergenerational church in Charlotte, North Carolina. Please pray for us. It is hard work.

What is your mission? Your mission is to proclaim "the excellencies of Him who called you out of darkness into the marvelous light." In the Hebraic understanding of the faith, "to proclaim" expresses the reality of living in harmony with God. This is not a one-time decision but an ongoing, moment-by-moment relationship with God. Through the infusion of grace and the power of the Holy Spirit, we become the Good News to our families and neighbors (Titus 2:11–14). Our lives begin to consistently reflect Jesus more and more at work, at school, in our parenting, in our singleness, in our repenting, in our suffering, in our doubt, in our conflict resolution, and in our play.

As the fragrance of His life emanates from us, we began the sacred work of engaging people verbally with the gospel (2 Corinthians 2:14–16). Some people will reject the Good News. Some people will receive the Good News. Either way, we proclaim "the excellencies of him who called you out of darkness into his marvelous light."

HEAD

- Reread Matthew 16:18.
- God's primary means of changing the world is through His community of people called the *ecclesia* (the Church).
- The Church is not a place you go on Sunday. The Church is Jesus' community of followers. It's His disciples. You are the Church!

HEART

- What feelings are being stirred in you as you read today's entry? Do you see the supreme importance of being the Church? How were you encouraged by this entry? How were you challenged by it? Write down your feelings and ask God to empower you to work through them.

HANDS

- Take a walk and wrestle with God. Pray for a passion to have a new understanding, appreciation, and involvement in your local church.
- Take some time to learn about what God is doing through His people all over the world. Check out www.BGEA.org or www.sim.org.

TWENTY-EIGHT

HERO, YOU ARE VALUABLE TO THE *ECCLESIA*

The human body has many parts, but the many parts make up one whole body. So it is with the body of Christ.

1 CORINTHIANS 12:12 NLT

LIVING STONES | A Spartan king bragged to a visiting emperor about the great and impenetrable walls of his city. Looking around, the esteemed guest could see no walls. Therefore he asked the Spartan king, "Where are these walls that you boast about so much?" The Spartan king looked into the eyes of his guest and pointed at his bodyguard and the multitudes of his highly skilled, battle-tested warriors. In the voice of a wise and experienced warrior, he said, "These men are the walls of Sparta; every man is a brick. These great men are the great walls of Sparta." The guest did not miss the king's point.

A solo brick is useless. It becomes useful when it is incorporated into a building with other bricks; this is also true for individual Christ-followers as well. Each Christ-follower is a "living stone" that is "being built up into a spiritual house" (1 Peter 2:5). The student of Jesus only realizes his destiny when he is built into the fabric of the local church.

The life of a disciple is a life of community.

It is a life of serving and a life of being served.

CONNECT, COMMIT, CONTRIBUTE | One of the great strengths of historic, biblical Christianity is that salvation is not found in an organization or denomination. It is found in the person of Jesus, the Son of God. One of the great weaknesses of historic, biblical Christianity is that we do not understand the value of being connected, committed, and contributors to a local community of faith. It is time we stop asking, "What can the church do for me and my needs?" This is consumerism. This is unheroic. The season is upon us that we must starting praying, "Holy Spirit, show me the way to a local community where I can get connected, be committed, and contribute my gifts." This is biblical. This is heroic.

T.E.A.M. | *Together Everyone Achieves More.*

The best football teams I played on in high school, college, and in the NFL had one thing in common: These great teams played as a unified, selfless, integrated team. Every player was valuable to the success of the team. Those teams understood that together everyone achieves more.

During the 1995–1996 NFL Season, I was one of four team captains for the Indianapolis Colts. No one expected much out of us as a team... except for the guys in the locker room. As the season progressed, players began to see that it did not matter who got their name in the paper or who was interviewed on ESPN's *Sports Center* after a victory. This sacrificial commitment to the "together everyone achieves more" philosophy paid off when the defending Super Bowl Champion, the San Francisco 49ers, came to town. Their roster was jam-packed with future NFL Hall of Fame players like Jerry Rice and Steve Young. The so-called experts said they would kill us.

For sixty minutes we battled like gladiators.

For sixty minutes we emptied ourselves out, believing that together everyone achieves more.

After the sixty minutes expired, we found ourselves victorious, 18–17. And yours truly intercepted quarterback Steve Young to set up a crucial field goal. I was able to make that big momentum-shifting play because my ten teammates on defense were executing their assignments.

Together everyone achieves more.

What I remember most about the game is how every player had a sense that what they did mattered...even if they did not play much on the actual game day. The scout team knew that in practice, as they demonstrated the 49ers offensive, defensive, and special-team plays, they were preparing the men who were going to play a significant portion of the game. We knew that together everyone would achieve more.

That season, a bunch of underestimated men believed that if we played as a unified, selfless, integrated team, we could have a special season. And we did. In the last seconds of the 1995–1996 AFC Championship game, our dream came to an agonizing end. The Pittsburgh Steelers were the better team. But through this experience, the Great Hero taught me a lesson of greater value than winning the Super Bowl: When people place their individual goals aside and sacrifice for others, together everyone achieves more.

As a disciple of Jesus, and as a young pastor, I take this same lesson and apply it to the kingdom of God. When the Great Hero's people, the Church, live as a unified, selfless, integrated team, together everyone achieves more.

CREATED FOR MINISTRY | God the Holy Spirit has gifted you to serve your local church and your community. Reflect prayerfully on this text:

> As each has received a gift, use it to serve one another, as good stewards of God's varied grace: whoever speaks, as one who speaks oracles of God; whoever serves, as one who serves by the strength that God supplies—in order that in everything God may be glorified through Jesus Christ. To him belong glory and dominion forever and ever. Amen (1 Peter 4:10–11 ESV).

God gives you gifts and even supplies the power to use those gifts to serve others. Why? So He can be made famous through our lives. When you do not use your Spirit-enabled gifts to bless others, it dishonors God and cripples your local church and community. It also gives you a lack of purpose.

America is the land of entertainment, yet many of us are bored with life. Could it be because we are not using our ministry gifts? You have been born during this time and in your sphere of influence to change the world through the gifts you have been given. You have been gifted for the good of the church and for the sake of the world (1 Corinthians 12:7). At the judgment seat of Christ, the King of glory will ask you, "How did you use the gifts I gave you to serve others?" (1 Corinthians 3:9–15). May you be able to say that day, "I used them well."

*It is validating to know that I have been created to do
some things well, and it's okay that I don't do other
things well. God created others to do those things,
and we are a team.*

V. Gray

If you do not know what your gifts are, ask a mature Christ-follower to help you to discover them. The way I discovered my ministry gifts was by volunteering at church. As you serve, your gifts will emerge. I also took a spiritual gift test, which would be available at your local Christian bookstore. This test helps you consider your strengths in spiritual tasks such as leading, giving, serving, and showing mercy.

NO LITTLE PEOPLE | There are no little people in the kingdom. Every ministry is vitally important (1 Corinthians 12:14–31). As a pastor, is it humbling to see how our community of faith impacts the city of Charlotte. The people in our congregation are coming alive as they see themselves as vital members of God's kingdom. An example of this is the team of people we have that lead the Montclaire Project. We have adopted an inner-city, at-risk elementary school where 90 percent of the students are on free or reduced lunch, an indicator of poverty levels. Many live in single-parent homes. The people in our church serve this school by giving the teachers appreciation gifts, chaperoning dances, being lunch buddies with the kids, and helping raise money to send the entire fifth grade to Washington, D.C. I wish you could have been there to see the faces of those students as they boarded a bus to go to our nation's capital.

*I want my children to be so rooted in the love of Christ that
they know their value is in who God says they are, not in
what they do. Lord, empower me to parent in such a way that
my children see using their gifts as heroic!*

V. Gray

DEPENDENT | My grandmother died of cancer. This terrible disease shut down her organs. In the same way, when you do not connect, commit, and contribute your gifts to your local church, that local church community suffers organ failure. Each member is dependent upon each other (1 Corinthians 12:21–26; Romans 12:5). When you do get involved, through the Holy Spirit's power, "the whole body, joined and held together by every joint with which it is equipped, when each part is working properly, makes the body grow so that it builds itself up in love" (Ephesians 4:16 ESV).

Together everyone achieves more.

HEAD

- Read Ephesians 4:11–16 and 1 Corinthians 12:1–31 using *lectio divina*. (See entry 24 to refresh your memory on this study method.)
- The Spirit of God has given you ministry gifts for the good of the church, for the sake of the world, and for your joy. It's time to use them!

HEART

- What feelings are surfacing in you as you read today's entry? How has your view of the Church and your vital role in it changed? How is this challenging? Record your feelings and ask God to empower you to work through them.

HANDS

- Get connected, committed, and contribute. If you are not connected, committed, and contributing to a local community of faith, ask the Holy Spirit to guide you to a community of Christ-followers. If you are connected to a local community of faith, prayerfully seek ways to use your gifts. Your gifts are valuable!
- Take a spiritual gifts assessment test.

TWENTY-NINE

HERO, LOVE YOUR WIFE WITH A JESUS KIND OF LOVE, PART I

However, let each one of you love his wife as himself,
and let the wife see that she respects her husband.

EPHESIANS 5:33 ESV

SINGLES, WHAT I AM WRITING IS FOR YOU, TOO ❘ This will help you prepare for marriage. Or, if you remain single, you can guide your married friends toward this advice and these resources.

I SHOULD NOT BE WRITING THIS... ❘ I should not be writing this entry about marriage. No one in my immediate family is married. For me, my brothers and sisters, and for many of my cousins, our lives were fractured because we missed out on having a father in our lives to model manhood for us. I mean no disrespect to my family. They are the only family I have, and I love them. But this is the sad reality.

As a teenager, I had no dreams of my wedding day. During a conversation with my grandmother, she mentioned in passing that she and my grandfather were married; I was seventeen years old when I learned that my grandparents were actually married. The first wedding I ever went to was my own at age twenty-one!

But through the Great Hero's grace, He has lifted me and my marriage on the wings of His love. He will do the same for you and your marriage, regardless of your background.

MARRIED AND CLUELESS | My bride and I were married as college students on May 23, 1992, in Provo, Utah. Our wedding cost about $800. We were poor and didn't mind that our wedding was inexpensive. When we said "I do," we had no idea that we were also saying "I do" to the dysfunction of our history. My wife's biological parents were divorced when she was five, so she entered into our marriage with security and self-esteem issues. And I brought along my junk, as well.

The early years of our marriage were characterized by me not being able to love Vicki the way she needed to be loved. Men, pause for a moment. If you have a daughter, as I do, how would you like to have your future son-in-law write those words about your little girl? One of the reasons I am writing this book is so there can be a man out there who is ready to sacrificially love my daughter the way she needs to be loved. And more importantly, the way Christ *commands* and *empowers* him to love (Ephesians 5:25). This goes for your daughters as well.

On the other side, my wife had no clue how to respect me, either. So here's the deal: I did not know how to love her, and she did not know how to respect me. This is a critical issue within a marriage relationship, and I will address it more in the coming entries. My philosophy on this subject has been largely inspired by my friend Dr. Emerson Eggerichs, author of the best-selling book, *Love and Respect*.

Neither my wife nor I were students of Jesus before we were married. It was not until the fall of 1997 that we became His followers. We probably would have been divorced by then if I were an uptight, domineering kind of guy. I'm pretty laid-back, so I would not engage in arguments—I would just give her the silent treatment. Things would blow over and we would continue with life. But what we thought blew over was instead being buried in our souls, creating bitterness and anger—key ingredients to an unhealthy marriage. By the time we had been married about five years, we were more like glorified roommates than loving married partners.

As we began to encounter Jesus through scripture, a deep and painful shift was taking place in both of us. As the Spirit of God gave me eyes to see my bride for the gift she was, I realized I did not have the resources to love her. The more I tried, the more I failed. I was a broken man. I pleaded with Jesus, "Love her through me because I do not know how." Everything changed after that prayer.

Our children are watching our marriage. Am I teaching them what a godly marriage looks like? Do I focus more on having my own needs met, or do I set my eyes on Christ and ask how I can sacrificially meet the needs of my husband?

V. Gray

A WEEKEND TO REMEMBER | In 2002, my wife and I were invited to a "Weekend to Remember" marriage conference presented by Dennis Rainey's Family Life Ministry. For two days we sat in silent awe of what we were learning about marriage. We realized that our marriage could be beautiful. We realized that God wanted us to have more than just a good marriage— He wanted and supplied the power to have a God-glorifying, soul-satisfying, heroic marriage. That's what we wanted.

A volcano of passion and thirst to be a heroic husband captured my imagination. Since that time, my wife and I have developed a saying when it comes to marriage: *The grass is greener where it is watered and fertilized.* For your marriage to be green and full of life, you—by the power of God that is housed in you—must water and fertilize it. What does that practically mean? For my bride and me, part of that caretaking is that we read a book on marriage, teach a seminar on marriage, or attend a marriage conference every other year.

People will often say to us, "You have a great marriage; why are you going to a marriage conference?" That question is like asking Michael Phelps, the great Olympic champion swimmer and world record holder, "Why do you train so hard in the swimming pool? You're a great swimmer." He trains hard to become an even greater swimmer. My bride and I do these things because we want to have a *heroic marriage*. Does this mean that we do not have problems in our marriage? Of course not! We've learned, and are still learning, how to work through our problems through the Holy Spirit's power.

Men, perhaps you are saying, "Derwin, I just don't have time." What are you so busy doing that you cannot make your marriage a priority? Maybe the evil one is keeping you busy so you can't take time to water and fertilize your marriage. Or maybe you keep busy so you will not have to deal with the problems in your marriage. It's time to step up to the plate. There is too much at stake. You are a legacy-builder.

In my next entry, we will look at some practical steps you can take to show your wife that you love her.

HEAD

- ❧ You are commanded and empowered by Jesus to love your wife in a sacrificial way (Ephesians 5:25, 33).
- ❧ The grass is greener where it is watered and fertilized. You must, by God's grace, train for marriage success.
- ❧ As a husband, you are a legacy-builder.

HEART

- ❧ What feelings are being stirred in you as you read today's entry? How do you show your wife you love her? Do you feel respected by her? Did this entry challenge you? Did it encourage you? Write down your feelings and ask God to empower you to work through them.

HANDS

- ❧ Start praying with your wife. Use the entry on the Disciples' Prayer as a guide (entry 25).
- ❧ Take your bride to a marriage conference. "Love and Respect" by Dr. Emerson and Sarah Eggerichs (www.loveandrespect.com) and Dennis and Barbara Rainey's "Weekend to Remember" (www.familylife.com) are two that my wife and I have greatly benefited from.
- ❧ Read this entry with your wife.

THIRTY

HERO, LOVE YOUR WIFE WITH A JESUS KIND OF LOVE, PART II

*However, let each one of you love his wife as himself,
and let the wife see that she respects her husband.*

EPHESIANS 5:33 ESV

AGAIN MY SINGLE FRIENDS, WHAT I AM WRITING IS FOR YOU, TOO | The sacredness of marriage is not for the understanding of married people only. According to God's love letter to us, marriage is a reminder of Jesus love for the Church (Ephesians 5:25–33).

BATTERIES INCLUDED | I have never understood why toys that require batteries do not include them in the package when you buy one. When I buy my son Jeremiah a remote control car, we are ready to drive it *now*—but we can't, because it doesn't come with batteries. Men, when you embraced Jesus and His *eternal kind of life*, He regenerated your soul, and the batteries were included. You can live *now* in His power; you do not have to wait until heaven. God inserted His spiritual batteries in you at your spiritual birth. That means you can love your bride *now*. Savor this soul-igniting truth:

> Blessed be the God and Father of our Lord Jesus Christ, who has blessed us in Christ with every spiritually blessing in the heavenly places (Ephesians 1:3 ESV).

So here's the deal: Men, *you have every spiritual blessing in Christ*. This means you have all the power you will ever need to love your wife. You have that power because the One who is full of power inhabits your soul. As we look at these practical steps of how to love your wife, remember this is worship, not mindless things you do. When you love your wife, even when she does not respect you, you are doing it in God's power for God's glory. My greatest ministry is not preaching or writing books. It is loving my wife. I am a failure and a fraud if I do not love my wife. Heroes, let's get to some lovin'!

INTIMACY: IN-TO-ME-YOU-SEE | Your wife feels loved when you are intimate with her. Stop doing backflips! In this context, I do not necessarily mean sexual intimacy. What I mean is that she desires for you to be close to her—emotionally, spiritually, and, yes, physically.

Study your wife. I want to earn a PhD in Vicki-ology. I want to know her. I am passionate about loving her in the way Jesus loves His Ecclesia (Ephesians 5:25). This is my bride…God's gift to me.

As you study your wife, you learn what her love languages are.[1] Is your wife energized by quality time, words of affirmation, gifts, acts of service, and/ or physical touch? My wife is energized by quality time, words of affirmation, and gifts. If you can list your favorite college or professional player's stats but not your wife's love languages, it is time for a radical priority shift. The Great Hero can do it in you. I know from experience…He's done it in me. And be patient with yourself; learning to study your wife is a lifelong journey.

Hold your wife's hand in public. This speaks the language of love to her. *And pay attention to her when she talks*. This means you listen with *24* or *Sports Center* turned off. Listen to her without looking down at your "Crackberry."

Men, pray with your wife. Grab her hand like the warrior-king you are and pray with her. Study your woman so you can have intimacy with her: In-to-me-you-see. She wants you to see into her.

SHARE YOUR FEELINGS | Your wife feels loved when you share your feelings with her. Talk to her about what you are experiencing. Early in my marriage, I thought it made me look weak to my wife if I shared my struggles and fears with her. It had the opposite effect. The more I opened up to her, the more she saw the man I could become.

Your wife wants to know what's going on in your world. If you are struggling at work, you are not protecting her by not letting her know. Bless her by letting her enter into your world with you. My wife is my best friend and counselor. I want her to know what I am feeling. She feels loved when I ask her to pray with me about my struggles. And so will your wife.

What are the things I can do that would make my husband want to love me this way? What are the things I am doing that put up a roadblock in front of my husband to keep him from wanting to love me this way?

V. Gray

JUST LISTEN | Your wife feels loved when you listen to her without trying to fix her problems. Hero-in-the-making, God has given you two ears and one mouth for a reason. Listen to your woman. Women talk to each other because they listen to each other. When she is sharing her struggles and problems with you, she does not want you to pull out your hammer and fix them. She wants you to listen and emotionally engage her as she processes what going on. I've learned through seventeen years of marriage to listen to my wife. As I listen, she processes her emotions and thoughts. And I'm the hero for listening.

Listening to her sends a love-message that says, "I value you enough to be present in your struggle." Never underestimate the power of listening. As you listen, repeat back to her, "What I hear you saying is…," and express how you heard her statements. This shows her that you are truly listening, and it can help you clarify if you have missed the point.

MOVE TOWARD HER | Your wife feels loved when you *move toward her in peace.* One of the most heroic things you can do is apologize to your wife when you are wrong or when you have hurt her with your words even when you are not wrong. You and your bride will argue. The key to resolving conflict in a godly way is to embrace and live out the truths of Section II in this book. You will become more and more secure in your identity in Jesus, and this will produce humility, which leads to the ability to say "I am sorry." As you move toward your wife in peace, she will feel loved.

DO YOU LOVE ME? | Your wife feels loved when she is secure in your loyalty to her. When your wife asks you, "Do you love me?" She is not asking for a lifeless statement. She is asking, "Are you loyal to me? Am I the only one you have eyes for? Am I safe with you, spiritually, emotionally, and physically?"

One of the most hurtful things you can ever do to your wife is for her to see you staring at another woman. It is like a thousand daggers being plunged into her heart all at once, especially if she has had your children and no longer looks as she used to. Brothers, in the power of the Holy Spirit, treasure your God and your wife by making a covenant with your eyes. Turn the TV station, fast-forward the movie scene, turn off the lingerie commercials—anything that would make your grandmother blush. There are times I will put my head down if an attractive woman walks by. I never, ever want my bride to feel as though she must compete with some twenty-two-year-old fitness expert who has not had children. I want my bride to feel as though she is the most beautiful and most fragrant-filled rose among the flowers.

Two more words of wisdom: *Do not joke in public about your wife.* This crushes her soul. And never, ever bring up the "D" word. Using divorce as a weapon leaves her feeling insecure.

TREASURE HER | Your wife feels loved when you treasure her. Talk to your children about how great your wife is. The kids love this. It gives them a sense of security, and it is modeling to your children what love in action looks like. Praise your wife for what she does. Let her know that you notice what she is doing, whether she works outside the home or not. My wife directs the day-to-day operations of our itinerant ministry, One Heart at a Time Ministries. Without her, we could not do and be all that God has created us to be.

Value and seek the opinion of your wife. Do not leave her in the dark on big decisions. So many times my wife has advised me with words of wisdom and encouragement. Your wife has abilities that you do not. Seek her opinion. You might save yourself a lot of pain, and gain a lot of wisdom. God has given her to you as your helpmate (Genesis 2:18).

Your bride loves it when you brag about her in public. Let her know that you are a team and what she does is equally as important as what you do. And one last thing…in an argument, please do not use the venomous phrase, "It's my money." No! It's God's money. And you are one flesh with your wife; therefore, the money you make with the ability God has blessed you with is for you and your bride to manage together.

DISPLAY JESUS | Men, I have provided you with some practical steps in how to show your wife that you love her. I am praying for you and your marriage. Your marriage is a walking advertisement to the world. Display Jesus well.

All right, women, you're next. We are going to look at practical ways you can show respect to your man. Get ready. You will be challenged.

HEAD

- Reread Ephesians 5:33.
- You can love your wife as Jesus loved His Church because you have "every spiritual blessing in Christ."
- Your greatest ministry is to love your wife.

HEART

- What are you feeling as you read today's entry? Have you loved your wife the way Jesus commands and empowers you to love her? If not, why? Write down your feelings and ask God to help you to work through them.

HANDS

- Tonight, read this entry with your wife. Ask her how you can show love to her. Write down what she communicates to you.
- Remember, you have every spiritual blessing in Christ. You can do this because Jesus will do it through you.
- Share what you are learning with other men, including your son(s).

THIRTY-ONE

HERO, HUSBANDS NEED A JESUS KIND OF RESPECT

However, let each one of you love his wife as himself,
and let the wife see that she respects her husband.

Ephesians 5:33 esv

THIS ENTRY IS FOR ALL READERS—MEN, WOMEN, MARRIED, OR SINGLE |
Everything I have written concerning Jesus, and the "eternal kind of life"
that He freely gives, applies to women as well as men. I pray that one day my
daughter, Presley, and her friends would read this book and be encouraged
to live a heroic life.

WOMEN ARE HEROES, TOO | *Women, you are created to live a heroic life!*
To live that life will require you to fight for it!

And for those of you that are married, your husband is your friend and
fellow warrior in the Great Hero's army of grace. One way the evil one and
his dark forces can derail your faith is through wrecking your marriage.

Ephesians 5:22–33 is a controversial section of scripture. What does
it mean to "submit" to your husband, and what does it mean to "respect"
your husband (Ephesians 5:22–24, 33)? For centuries, many men have
used this section of scripture to dominate, abuse, and treat their wives in
an unheroic way. This is one unhealthy extreme; however, in recent years,
another unhealthy extreme has emerged: Women are not mentored in the
biblical and beautiful understanding of what it means to submit to and
respect their husbands.

SUBMISSION AND RESPECT | My bride has a great definition of what biblical submission is: It is refusing to take control. Just as the Church submits to Jesus as its servant-leader, wives should also submit out of love and respect to their husband's God-ordained servant-leadership role. You are probably yelling at this point, "Pastor D. Gray, my husband is not a servant-leader.... If I do not take control, nothing gets done!" I will give you another Vicki-ism, "Duck, and let the Holy Spirit swing and knock Him to his knees." Your taking control and nagging him will not change him, but a right hook from God can (Psalm 119:67, 71). Trust me…I know from experience.

And ladies, respect does not mean that you live as a doormat. It does mean that you honor your husband, even when he does not deserve it. Yes, you read that last sentence correctly. Just as your husband is commanded and empowered to love you even when you do not deserve it, you are likewise commanded and empowered to respect your husband even when he does not deserve it.

Can you imagine your husband telling you, "I will give you the love you need when you earn it"? That would be emotional abuse. It is also emotional abuse when you tell your husband through your words and actions, "I will respect you when you earn it." In our twisted culture, it is "okay" for a woman to have this attitude. But if a man had that attitude, he would be called names I cannot write.

Let me be clear. Respecting your husband does not mean that you enable sinful behavior like alcoholism, adultery, physical abuse, or porn addiction. I have seen women enable these sin patterns in their husband's lives to the detriment of their marriages and families. We will take a look in a minute at how you can show respect to your husband in practical and encouraging ways.

LOVE COMES NATURALLY | Love comes naturally to women; respect does not. Women, for the most part, are nurturers. Your natural inclination is to love your husband. He knows that you love him. He's just not sure that you like or respect him. When you disrespect him, you are crushing his manhood. During an argument, when he withdraws and gives you the silent treatment, it's because he does not want to show you the disrespect you are showing him.

Women, how would you feel if your future daughter-in-law talked to your son with the disrespect in which you talk to his father? Think about it. Not a pretty sight, is it?

BUT, DERWIN... | Perhaps you are thinking, "But, Derwin, you don't know what he has done to hurt me." You're right. I don't know what he has done. But I do know what Jesus has done to heal broken marriages. As my best friend and bride said during a marriage seminar we were teaching, "Adultery is grounds for divorce. But it is also grounds for forgiveness." There is nothing that Jesus and His gospel cannot overcome.

_____

Once the realization hits that we must unconditionally respect our husbands, we must also realize that God does not expect us to do this in our own strength. In fact, as those who love Christ, we have the power that raised Jesus from the dead living in us and through us!

V. Gray

_____

Ladies, I want to give you some practical steps that you can take to show your man the respect that he hungers for.

VALUE HIS PURSUITS | Your husband feels respected when you value his pursuits. He longs for you to be his biggest cheerleader. When my wife sends me a text or writes me a card encouraging me in my career, I feel incredible. It's like my heart explodes with love for her. As you show how you value his pursuits, your man will feel respected.

VALUE HIM AS PROTECTOR AND PROVIDER | Your husband feels respected when you value his position as your protector and provider. Praise him for being the family provider. Let him know that you are in his corner and that you believe in him.

Let him know that you feel secure in his care. When he sees how you have confidence in him as a protector and provider, he will be encouraged to live up to your regard for him.

Ladies, if you are the primary provider, please, please do not throw that in his face. It will crush him.

VALUE HIS ROLE AS SERVANT-LEADER | Your husband feels respected when you value his role as the family leader. Being the family leader is not a position of domination, but a position of servanthood. Jesus is the king of the universe, yet He was the world's greatest servant-leader. Your husband is the servant-leader of your family. Ladies, please take note: Your man cannot lead if you are trying to control him. He does not need another mother. He needs a wife that respects his God-given role as the servant-leader. Let him lead. I am the head of my family. My wife is the neck. Together we make a great team.

Another way to honor his servant-leadership is when you honor his authority in front of your children and others. When you do this, you are building him up *and* teaching your children how to have a healthy marriage… passing a blessing down to your kids. If you disrespect your husband in public, you are suffocating his spirit. He will begin to grow bitter toward you. And please do not nag him. Your nagging is not going to change him! Let God change him. When you honor his God-given role of servant-leadership, he will feel respected. And your children will see how a godly woman treats her husband.

This does not mean that you will not disagree with your husband. It *does* mean that you disagree in a way that is honoring. Besides, if you do that, you are likely to get your point across in a more effective way.

VALUE HIS INSIGHT | Your husband feels respected when you value his insight. As you engage him in conversation, let him know up front if you want him to help you figure out your problems or just listen. Give your husband permission to help you with your struggles by using his insight. God has given him the ability to fix things. Let him use that ability in your marriage. Make sure you thank him for his advice. This will make him feel respected.

VALUE AND SEEK RELATIONSHIP WITH HIM | Your husband feels respected when you value and seek relationship with him. One of the ways my wife shows respect for me is by lying on the couch with me and watching TV. We do nothing but chill. Early in our marriage, my wife could not sit still; she had to accomplish something. When she would not "chill" with me, I felt as if the things she needed to do were more important than me. As my security in Jesus grew, I shared my feelings with her. One night, she went to sleep on the couch with her hands clutching my bicep. As I looked at my queen sleeping, a wave of emotion arrested me. I felt respected.

Join your man in doing some of his hobbies. Our hobbies are golf and movies. Ladies, what are your man's hobbies? Engage. Make an effort to be interested in something that he is interested in. You may be amazed at how the lines of communication can open up when you share time doing something that you can both enjoy. A game of golf, a few hours fishing, or even a morning jog can be the gateway into your man's heart.

VALUE AND PURSUE HIM SEXUALLY | Your husband feels respected when you value and pursue him sexually. At the beginning of our marriage, sex was a source of contention. I wanted to have sex too much, and I felt like she did not want to have it enough. We have learned that the Great Hero even uses sex to make us more like Jesus. Several years ago, at the height of our contention over this issue, my wife and I prayed for God to decrease my desire and to increase her desire. As a result of this prayer, our sex life gets better every year…but more importantly, we have become servants to each other. Isn't that what the Great Hero is looking for?

When you pursue and initiate sex with your husband, he may have a heart attack…in a good way. Your man will feel respected. Trust me on this one. Try it and see what happens. Keep your marriage hot.

We live in an oversexed culture, so give him the freedom to let you know when he is struggling with sexual temptation. Do not make him feel ashamed. If you do that, he will hide his struggles in darkness, and what is in the dark, Satan can control. But what is in the light, Jesus controls.

As a married person, your body does not belong to you alone, but also to your spouse. Withholding sex from each other is a sin (1 Corinthians 7:1–5). Sex in the context of marriage is a sacred gift from God…something we can use for each other, not against each other.

LOVE AND RESPECT | Because you have "every spiritual blessing in Christ," you and your spouse can love and respect each other. Hero-man, as you love your wife unconditionally, you are honoring Jesus. Hero-woman, as you respect your husband unconditionally, you are honoring Jesus. Your marriage is a divine invitation to the people in your sphere of influence to taste and see that the Lord is good. Enjoy each other, friends! That's heroic. That's beautiful.

HEAD

- Read Ephesians 5:25–33 using *lectio divina* (entry 24).
- Women, you are commanded and empowered by Jesus to unconditionally respect your husband.
- Respecting your husband does not mean that you enable sinful habits. Encourage him in positive ways.

HEART

- What are you feeling as you read today's entry? Did it challenge you? Did it encourage you? Whether you are a man or woman, married or single, write down your feelings and ask God to empower you to work through them.

HANDS

- Married people, talk about this entry together.
- Wives, choose one suggestion from this entry to pursue this week. Don't tell your husband. Just do it.
- If you don't respect your husband, ask God to help you.

THIRTY-TWO

HERO, PARENTING MATTERS TO GOD

Children are a gift from the LORD; they are a reward from him.
PSALM 127:3 NLT

THE BLUE BUCKET | We hate blue buckets. When my wife was pregnant, she would vomit in the blue bucket…a lot. Not just in the morning, but all day, every day, for nine months. She had a medical condition that literally caused her to puke for nine months straight. Even while pushing during delivery, she would have to stop pushing so she could puke in the blue bucket. Ever had the flu before? That's what she felt like for nine months. Since she could not keep food down, she was hospitalized several times and intravenously fed by home nurses. That's why we hate blue buckets.

But as I watched her suffer and sacrifice to bring our children into the world, my love and admiration for her grew. The blue bucket is also a reminder of the gift that our children are from the Great Hero. Let's explore some practical ways we can appreciate children as the gift from God that they really are.

CHILDREN ARE A GIFT WITH GIFTS | Children are a gift from God (Psalm 127:3–5). With each passing year, I grow in my awareness of how awesome it is to be Presley's and Jeremiah's papa. Presley is gifted in the art of relationship, leadership, conversation, and creativity. It would not surprise me if she became a writer or an actress. Jeremiah is math-wise with a tender heart and out-of-this-world athletic ability. It would not surprise me if he became a professional athlete and pastor.

They are both unique.

They both have a purpose in the Great Story.

As parents, it is our privilege to walk alongside our children on their journey toward who God wants them to be…not who we want them to be. As parents, we are to train our children according to their God-wired ways, not our dreams for them (Proverbs 22:6). As parents, we are to guide them in mining for the treasure that God has deposited in their lives.

Do you have time to dig into the depths of who God has created your children to be? Some of the best times you will ever spend with your children are when you talk, study, and discover the gifts that your children are and uncover the gifts that God has placed within them.

WORSHIP OR NEGLECT | We are not called to worship our children. If we are not careful, we can turn our children into little gods: They get what they want when they want it. We schedule our days around them; they are like the sun and we are planets that revolve around them. Instead of being their parents, we become their servants. This produces selfish, disrespectful, narcissistic, entitlement-demanding adults who suck the life out of society.

Friends, please discipline your children (Proverbs 29:15). The freest people on earth are disciplined, which means they are trained in self-control and good conduct. As a parent, that is your calling: to train your children in the "eternal kind of life" as they learn to rely on the Spirit's power, and the best way to do that is by example. Titus 2:11–12 communicates this truth:

> For the grace of God has appeared, bringing salvation for all people, training us to renounce ungodliness and worldly passions, and to live self-controlled, upright, and godly lives in the present age (ESV).

Please do not release upon society undisciplined children.

The other extreme that I see is when parents neglect their children. Your children need you. How much time and energy do you have invested in your children? It is great that you provide for them physically, but they need you to be present in their lives. For the last seven years, I have read to my children's classes. Do I have time? Yes…only because I make time to do it. I want to be present in their lives.

_____

Sometimes the extremes go hand-in-hand: The father works so hard to provide that he neglects the family; the mom's life revolves around the children; the marriage becomes less of a priority. Lord, we need You to teach us balance on a continual basis!

V. Gray

_____

TEACHING THE FAITH | Dads and moms, it is your privilege to teach your children the faith (Deuteronomy 6:4–9). While they may come alongside to help you, your church's children's director or youth pastor's job is not to teach your children the faith. It is yours.

> You shall bind them as a sign on your hand, and they shall be as frontlets between your eyes. You shall write them on the doorposts of your house and on your gates (Deuteronomy 6:8–9 ESV).

Cultivating young heroes is bound up in your actions ("hand") and attitudes ("head"), and it must be inscribed in our private lives ("doorposts") and our public lives ("gates").[1] This does not mean you are perfect. You will not be, and neither am I. It does mean that we join God in developing our children into Christ-followers.

Do all that is in your power. As they come of age, they must choose whether they will walk with the Great Hero. You can be the greatest parent in the world and your children may not follow Jesus. God calls you to remain faithful, regardless of the outcome. Trust Him for the ultimate results.

Family devotions. If you are like me, family devotions are like a WWE match. You pull out your family devo, you pray, and then the kids start a wrestling match. Presley gets Jeremiah in a headlock. He tackles her like a blitzing Troy Polamalu, and my wife and I look at each other, thinking, "Lord, what have we done to deserve this torture?"

A few years ago, we started viewing our daily life as our family devotions. Sure, we have times of prayer and scripture reading as a family. Presley works through a curriculum for her youth group, and Jeremiah and I read through a kid's Bible. But now we do not limit our instruction to a morning quiet time; we teach our kids that school is their mission field and that difficult relationships are God's gymnasium for spiritual formation. We teach them that studying for a test is worship and obeying their teachers is worship. The verses above from Deuteronomy teach that parenting and teaching the faith are a way of life built into the fabric of daily life.

WHAT CHILDREN NEED FROM THEIR PAPA[2] | *Papa, I cannot hear "I love you" enough.* Dads, your children need and long to hear you say, "I love you." You can never say "I love you" enough. As a boy, I never had a father say, "Son, I love you," so I rain down "I love yous" on Presley and Jeremiah. May the words "I love you" echo in their souls long after they leave your home.

Papa, show me your love. Children spell love "T-I-M-E." For me, "pastor, author, and speaker" are secondary roles to "husband and father." In light of my priorities, I delegate my time accordingly. I coach my son's football teams and make the majority of the games my daughter cheerleads. I also go on dates with my daughter, which include shopping at Claire's and Juicy Couture. Yes, men, I go into these girly stores with my head held high. I share this with you not to show you that I have it together—I do not. I simply want to encourage you that you can give your children the papa-time they need.

Papa, will you be my friend, too? The demands of life can crush our ability to have fun, can't it? As a result, our fun-meter becomes damaged and we lose the ability to have fun with our children. Let's not let our children have memories of Dad always being tired and not having enough energy to be their friend and do fun things.

Papa, you will always be my hero. Men, even in the teenage years when it seems like your children are distant, they still see you as their hero. God has given us men a special place in our children's heart that says, "Dad, you will always be my hero." For example, my daughter, Presley, is maturing into a teenager. She does not hang out with me like she used to. But on road trips when she travels with me to my preaching engagements, my "wingman" opens up and we have incredible conversations. Papa is still her hero.

Papa, please listen to me. Through the years of speaking across America to students, I know they have shared deep secrets with me they do not share with their parents. They said the reason is because I listen. Now here's the hard part for me. I find it easier to listen to other people's children then my own. I am continually asking for the power to be a listener when my kids are sharing what's happening in their lives. So before we start giving advice, let's listen to our children. This means listening with the TV and "Crackberry" off. Look them in the eyes and listen. Listening says "I love you."

Papa, keep it real with me. One of the greatest gifts you can give your children is your story. Life is hard, and they need to know how life has beaten you up at times. They need to know that you are not perfect. Talk about the regrets of your past mistakes.

Papa, I need you to coach me. As my children get older, I see myself coaching them more. A coach is an experienced guide who offers advice on the issues of life. The best coaches tend to be the ones that teach out of their life experiences. Share with your children how you reacted in a similar situation they are experiencing.

Papa, help me develop my identity. Our children are constantly being bombarded with images and words that are trying to shape who they will become. It is our calling to constantly remind them of who they are in Christ. Their value, self-meaning, love, and mission for life are anchored in Jesus, not friends, school, the clothes they wear, or their career choices, but in Jesus alone. And some of the greatest times to remind them of this truth are in the midst of heartache and suffering. During these times of brokenness, they are more open to embrace who they are in Christ.

PARENTING TAKES COURAGE | Let's be heroic parents and join the Great Hero in growing heroic children. We can do it...because we have every spiritual blessing in Christ (Ephesians 1:3).

HEAD

❧ Read Psalms 127:3–5 and Deuteronomy 6:4–9 using *lectio divina* (entry 24). Children are gifts from God.

❧ Your children have gifts from God. You are called to guide them in mining their souls and discovering their gifts.

❧ It is your calling to teach your children the faith.

HEART

❧ What feelings are you experiencing as you read today's entry? What do you remember about your relationship with your parents? How did they help you to discover your gifts? How did they teach you the faith? Have you forgiven your parents? Write down your feelings and ask God to empower you to work through them.

HANDS

❧ Tell your child "I love you" today and every day this week.

❧ Start praying for your children—for their futures, their attitudes, their friends, and their faith.

❧ Let your child see you reading the Bible or praying this week.

THIRTY-THREE

HERO, THERE IS HEROIC SINGLE LIVING

For in Christ lives all the fullness of God in a human body. So you also are complete through your union with Christ, who is the head over every ruler and authority.

COLOSSIANS 2:9–10 NLT

MARRIED PEOPLE, PLEASE READ THIS ENTRY! | As you read, pray that the Holy Spirit will allow you to use it to encourage and counsel your single friends. Perhaps one day you may use this entry to mentor your children. You may even find it useful as you consider what your marital status means to you.

PHILIP'S STORY | Philip wanted to get married. All of his college friends were getting married. The buddies he used to hang out with on Friday nights were now hanging out with their wives.

He felt incomplete.

He was lonely.

He felt purposeless.

As I mentored him through this season, we identified several lies he and many singles believe that led down the highway of despair.

LIE #1 | *I am incomplete if I do not have a spouse.* A spouse will not and cannot complete you. I tell my bride often, "Baby, Big Papa cannot love you like Jesus." She says, "I know; that's why I worship him and not you...which gives me the power to put up with you." Singles, my wife does not complete me, and I do not complete her. My connectedness to Jesus completes me

(Colossians 2:10). And your connectedness to Jesus completes you. If you think your spouse will complete you, you will turn that person into a little god, and little gods always disappoint. You will set expectations for your future spouse that they can never live up to. Your unrealistic expectations will be like a straitjacket to them.

In a painful but necessary conversation, I told Philip, "You want a wife more than you want Jesus. God is sparing you right now by not bringing you a wife. If you had a wife, you would turn her into a little god. When you begin journeying toward finding your completeness in Christ, then you will have the resources to love a wife."

LIE #2 | *If I have a spouse, I will not be lonely anymore.* Out of desperation, many singles marry the wrong person for the wrong reason. Friends, it is better to be lonely and alone than to be married to the wrong person and still be lonely. I have seen married people lonely. I have seen single people lonely. There are seasons of loneliness for everyone. Could it be that God may be using your loneliness to draw you closer to Him?

Singles, I have empathy for you. I've journeyed with enough singles to know that it is hard. If you are not married by age twenty-six, it feels like people are thinking, "What's wrong with you?" and of course, everyone tries to hook you up with a date, right? Jesus never said life would be easy, but He did say "I will be with you."

One of the most soul-shrinking habits you can develop is hanging out solely in a community of other singles whose main focus is centered on being single. As you dwell on being not married, it will be begin to eat away at your soul.

Instead of focusing on what you do not have, focus on everything God has given you. One of the ways to do that is by participating in an intergenerational community. People that are diverse in age and marital status can cross-pollinate your spiritual growth. You can learn from married couples. You can learn from divorced people. You can learn from older people who have been single for fifty years. Here's the deal: Get your eyes off yourself and look to the Great Hero (Colossians 3:1–3). Will this be easy? No, but it will be heroic.

LIE #3 | *I do not have a purpose because I am not married.* You are not without purpose! You are not defined by your singleness. You are defined by your God, who has given you a role in His Great Story.

While working out at the YMCA I met a woman named Angela. I asked her to come and check out our church. She said, "I would not fit in." I asked her why. She said it was because she was divorced. I looked her in the eyes and said, "Your being divorced does not define you. You are a daughter of the King. You are deeply loved and accepted by Him. What defines you is the fact that you are a child of God."

She looked at me like I had two heads; she was stunned. For so long she'd bought the lie that she was defined by being single and divorced. Eventually she joined our church and is now the children's ministry director.

———

Who are the singles in my sphere of influence that I can love, mentor, and encourage? How am I preparing my children to understand that Christ completes them and a member of the opposite sex does not?

V. Gray

———

Whether you are married or single, you are called to play your role in the Great Story by partnering with God in making disciples and loving the people in your sphere of influence (Matthew 28:18–20). As a single, you have ministry opportunities that a married person will never have. There are things that you can do that I cannot do because I am married.

What opportunities are there for you to serve this broken planet that you have overlooked by focusing on what you do not have?

Celebrate your singleness!

And be honest with the Great Hero about your struggles. Are you content with God being enough? Do you hunger for a spouse more than you hunger for Jesus? Offer your struggles to Him and let His presence be enough to strengthen you.

You are valuable, and you have purpose—and that purpose is to be a hero!

BOY MEETS GIRL | I encouraged Philip to desire Jesus more than anything else on earth. I also encouraged him to pray for a godly wife who could join him on mission with Jesus to heal this broken planet. As he responded to the Spirit of God, he humbly came to a place of saying, "Jesus, if I never get married, you are enough." Guess what happened? He met Geri. And then some time after that I performed Philip and Geri's wedding. It was awesome. What was most incredible to me was the soul-formation in Philip's life. I had cried with him before as he expressed his pain. I was now crying with him as he expressed his joy.

I am not saying that one day you will get married. But I am saying that today you can live a complete, purposeful, heroic life.

HEAD

- Reread Colossians 2:10. You are complete in Christ. A spouse does not complete you.

HEART

- What feelings are being stirred in you as you read today's entry? How did it challenge you? How did it encourage you? Record your feelings and ask God to empower you to work through them.

HANDS

- Get involved in an intergenerational community.
- Explore opportunities to serve and use your ministry gifts in your local church and your community. At-risk schools could use lunch buddies or classroom readers. Are there oversees mission trips you can go on? Notice the needs around you and take action.
- If you want to get married, pray through the lies and discover your role in God's Great Story. Then pray for a godly spouse that will join you on mission!

THIRTY-FOUR

HERO, PURSUE THE TRUE TREASURE, PART I

"For where your treasure is, there your heart will be also."
MATTHEW 6:21 ESV

SATAN IS NOT GOING TO LIKE THIS | For Christ-followers in America, Satan knows that money and possessions are how he can wreak havoc and distract us from living in the Great Story. Here's the deal: Having money and nice things is not evil. But when money and nice things have you, then there is a problem. The issue is your heart and what you treasure above all.

CONSUMERISM AND MATERIALISM | My definition of consumerism is this: when a person finds their identity, meaning, and purpose from what they buy and possess. I define materialism this way: when the good gifts God has given to us—like money, clothes, cars, homes, and others things—have dethroned God from His rightful place of leadership in our lives. Consumerism and materialism both mean that we begin to treasure God's good gifts more than God Himself.

Satan is on a relentless, reckless, and strategic mission to keep you from obeying Jesus' commands concerning money and possessions. Why? Because the way you and I use God's money and possessions is a declaration of our eternal values. What we do with the money God calls us to manage clearly affirms which kingdom we belong to. It is often said, "If you want to know if a man is committed to God's kingdom, look at how he is spending his money."

Whenever we use God's money and possessions for the advancement of His kingdom, we are casting a ballot for Jesus and against Satan, for heaven and against hell. Whenever we use God's money and God's possessions selfishly and indifferently, we advance Satan's kingdom of darkness. Did you read that? This is serious business! Too many Christ-followers have been suckered into the lie that money and possessions are ours to do with as we please without serious effect on life now or in eternity.

BUT, DERWIN... | Many of you are saying, "But, this is my money...these are my possessions." No, they are not! Not only does God own all of your money and possessions, He even owns you! Listen to God with your heart:

> The earth belongs to the LORD, and everything in it—the world and all its people. (Psalm 24:1 NCV).

> Do you not know that your body is a temple of the Holy Spirit within you, whom you have from God? You are not your own, for you were bought with a price. So glorify God in your body (1 Corinthians 6:19–20 ESV).

WHAT JESUS SAYS | In Matthew 6:19–21, Jesus teaches us about seeking the true treasure:

> Do not lay up for yourselves treasures on earth, where moth and rust destroy and where thieves break in and steal, but lay up for yourselves treasures in heaven, where neither moth nor rust destroys and where thieves do not break in and steal. For where your treasure is, there your heart will be also (ESV).

When you allow God's good gifts to dethrone Him as God, Jesus says moth and rust destroy them and thieves break in and steal. God, the Unrelenting Lover, is basically saying, "If you allow all these good things I gave you to become your treasure, you will be miserable."

A man dressed like a *GQ* fashion model sat down near me one day at Starbucks and began talking with his life coach.

He had designer hair,
> designer clothes,
>> designer shoes,
>>> and perfect teeth.

I couldn't help but overhear their conversation. After the life coach left, the *GQ* model look-alike, who I will call Henry, began to talk to me. I found out that Henry was a successful dentist…that explains the perfect teeth. Through the success of his dental practice he had the money, the girl, the house, and the cars. Like a big game hunter, he had captured and bagged the American dream. Yet he was meeting with a life coach because he was miserable! His treasure was money and possessions. He said to me, "I am miserable. My money, my stuff, define me…. I do not know who I am."

This is what Jesus means when he says "moth and rust destroy and where thieves break in and steal." Tragically, Henry was living an unheroic life.

IN PURSUIT OF TRUE TREASURE | Jesus says to treasure God and His kingdom above everything. When we progress in treasuring God above all else, we mature in how we use God's money and possessions. What does God treasure most? People!

The Great Hero's glory is most revealed when humanity treasures Him above all. God gives us His money and possessions to manage so that His will can be done on earth! Whether you make $1,000,000 a year or $20,000 a year, the issue is your heart and your willingness to say to Jesus, "I want to use Your money and possessions for what You treasure most."

MATERIALISM GONE WILD | As a nation, we are in the worst economic crisis since the Great Depression. As a nation and as individuals we lusted for what we did not have and bought it on credit when we could not afford it. The United States is the largest debtor nation in the world. As a people, we are in debt also. Some debt occurs because of unfortunate circumstances in life. But for a lot of people, their debt is because they were trying to keep up with the Joneses. Friends, even the Joneses have foreclosed. Instead of trying to keep up with the Joneses, let's walk in line with what Jesus says.

Materialism and greed have plunged our country into this economic dilemma because of our intoxicated eyes:

The eye is the lamp of the body. So, if your eye is healthy, your whole body will be full of light, but if your eye is bad, your whole body will be full of darkness. If then the light in you is darkness, how great is the darkness! (Matthew 6:22–23 ESV).

INTOXICATED EYES | When you compare yourself to someone else, you always lose. Pride or despair will overtake you. Be honest. How many of you base what you buy on God's will for your life, or do you base it on what other people have or what they will think about you? God created us to love people, and He has given us good gifts like money and possessions for His glory—but materialists love things and use people for their own glory.

———

Am I secure enough in who God says I am that I do not need to have the latest fashions, drive the nicest car, or have an impeccable house that impresses everyone who comes through the door? What do those who watch me see that I value?

———

V. Gray

The lust of materialism in America has become psychotic. Just about every commercial is trying to get you to purchase things you do not need. Corporations now sell their products in a way that promises a kind of salvation! Some car commercials entice you to believe that you not only get the car you can't afford, but you also get the five beautiful ladies in the commercial, too.

Once again, buying and having things we *need* is good. The problem occurs when we pursue and treasure things above and beyond their rightful place in our lives as servants, not masters. Can I get an "Amen?"

HERE'S THE DEAL |

No one can serve two masters, for either he will hate the one and love the other, or he will be devoted to the one and despise the other. You cannot serve God and money (Matthew 6:24 ESV).

Jesus said, "No one can serve two masters." The word *serve* means "slave." Do you feel enslaved by your debt? By your need to keep up appearances?

Marinate in the promise of this: *In becoming God's slave, you begin to experience freedom from commercialism and materialism.*

Jesus teaches you to seek the true treasure, which is Himself, because surveys show 85-90 percent of marriages that end in divorce cite money problems as the number one reason.[1] Jesus says "Treasure me, so you can be free."

He does not want you to have ulcers because you are worried about paying a mortgage on a home that was out of your price range to begin with. Jesus says, "Treasure me so you can be free."

Friends, money, and possessions make terrible masters, yet they make great servants in the hands of those who have the right master—God.

Hero, God has blessed you with money and possessions. Are you ready to use them for His honor, your joy, and the good of the world? If so, ask God to give you a heart to pursue and treasure Jesus above all.

HEAD

🌿 Prayerfully read Matthew 6.19–24.

🌿 What you do with the money and possessions you have affirms to which kingdom you belong. When you treasure Jesus, you will use His money and possessions to advance His kingdom.

HEART

🌿 What feelings are you experiencing as you read today's entry? Did it challenge you? Does the way you manage God's money and possessions reflect a commitment to His kingdom or yours? Write down your feelings and ask God to empower you to work through them.

HANDS

🌿 If you are married, review with your spouse how you spend money. If you are single, do this with a trusted friend.

🌿 See if your spending habits advance Jesus' kingdom.

🌿 Spend some time in prayer. Remember, conviction is from God, not guilt.

🌿 Think of ways you can use God's money and possessions to advance His kingdom.

THIRTY-FIVE

HERO, PURSUE THE TRUE TREASURE, PART II

"But seek first the kingdom of God and His righteousness, and all these things will be added to you."

MATTHEW 6:33 ESV

CAN WE TRUST GOD TO PROVIDE? | People in the congregation that I copastor are losing jobs weekly. In the worst economic crisis since the 1930s, there is the great fear in the deepest part of us that says: "God, if I treasure Jesus above all else and give You control of my money and possessions, can I trust You to meet my needs?" Friend, you can trust Jesus. He will meet your needs. But here is the kingdom-of-God reality: He meets your needs so that you can meet the needs of others.

JESUS SPEAKS |

> "Therefore I tell you, do not be anxious about your life, what you will eat or what you will drink, nor about your body, what you will put on. Is not life more than food, and the body more than clothing? Look at the birds of the air: they neither sow nor reap nor gather into barns, and yet your heavenly Father feeds them. Are you not of more value than they? And which of you by being anxious can add a single hour to his span of life? And why are you anxious about clothing? Consider the lilies of the field, how they grow: they neither toil nor spin, yet I tell you, even Solomon in all his glory was not arrayed like one of these. But if God so clothes the grass of the field, which today is alive and tomorrow is thrown into the oven, will he not much more clothe you, O you of

little faith? Therefore do not be anxious, saying, 'What shall we eat?' or 'What shall we drink?' or 'What shall we wear?' For the Gentiles seek after all these things, and your heavenly Father knows that you need them all. But seek first the kingdom of God and his righteousness, and all these things will be added to you. Therefore do not be anxious about tomorrow, for tomorrow will be anxious for itself. Sufficient for the day is its own trouble" (Matthew 6:25-34 ESV).

When Jesus tells us to consider how the Great Hero provides for the birds of the air and the lilies of the field, He is not giving you a license to be irresponsible—just the freedom to trust God to provide for your life. The Jewish audience that Jesus was talking to was familiar with this attitude toward life. Many rabbis in Jesus' day taught that a man ought to meet life with a combination of good sense, a strong work ethic, and a reliance on God. They believed that every man must teach his son a trade. If they did not do this, they were teaching him to steal. With equal passion and commitment, they believed that God would provide for their basic needs.

AN EXAMPLE | If you have lost your job, like I did when the Carolina Panthers fired me in 1998, sitting at home and waiting for a job to magically appear is not what Jesus is teaching. He teaches us to worship Him by preparing the best resumé possible, to work every connection you have, and, most importantly, to pray that you land a job where you can be the Good News to your new work environment. Be tenacious.

BUDGET | Do you have any clue how much money you spend each month?

How are you doing with the management of God's money?

He has not given you the ability to earn money just so you can have it to do with as you please. It's His money, in your hands, for His glory. As Christ-followers, we usually go to extremes when it comes to money. One extreme is the vow of poverty. The thought goes like this: If you take a vow of poverty, then you are really spiritual. A person can take a vow of poverty and be a million, trillion light-years away from God spiritually.

The other extreme is the "name-it-and-claim-it" nonsense of the so-called "prosperity gospel," which is no gospel at all. In this perversion they say God desires for His people to be healthy and wealthy. And if you are not healthy and wealthy, you do not have enough faith. God is at the whim of whatever you want. He's a giant ATM in the sky. Try telling that nonsense to Christ-followers in China or a third-world nation who live with great faith yet are not wealthy and many are not healthy. But more importantly, they are rich in faith and healthy in kingdom-living.

So do you have a budget? I strongly recommend that you develop one. My wife and I have one. Please do not assume that we "have it together"; we do not. We do desire to manage God's money as best we can. That's why we work hard at having a financial strategy. Developing a budget is an act of worship. As my wife and I have seen in our lives, a budget can help you effectively use God's money for the advancement of His kingdom.

ARE YOU A GENEROUS GIVER? | How much of God's money do you give to your local community of faith and other ministries? Let me take off the gloves. What I am about say is not given in condemnation, but in a divine invitation. Many of you have been seduced, used, and abused by consumerism and materialism so badly that each month you give more to paying off credit card debt from buying things you could not afford than you do for the furthering of God's kingdom. This needs to cease. I know there are special cases where emergency pushes us into debt. I'm not talking about those rare cases. Friends, Satan desires to keep you bound to consumerism and materialism. He does not want you to treasure Jesus. If you did, your money would make a greater impact in the world and you would experience more freedom.

Something is always breaking, going out of style, or is just never enough. Worshiping possessions makes me miserable! Lord, thank You for allowing all of these things to fail me so that I will worship You, the one true and living God!

V. Gray

WORRY | In verse 32, Jesus teaches us that if we worry about God meeting our basic needs, we are acting like people who worship pagan gods. Pagan gods are a moody bunch; they are never satisfied. Those who worship these false gods are in constant anxiety because they cannot be relied upon, and one never knows when they are happy.

Several years ago, I was asked to pray for a Christian man who had lost his job. When I entered his home, a vomit-prompting smell hit me like a blitzing linebacker. Sadly, the smell was him! He had not showered in about two weeks. He just would lie in his bed all day with the covers over his whole body, except for his eyes. As I talked with him, all he could say was, "I can't pay my bills. I can't fix my house. I lost my job." His anxiety overtook him.

About a week later, as friends continued to pray for him and speak the truth of Matthew 6:33 to him, he eventually got back on his feet. He is now a successful businessman.

SEEKING: WHAT DOES IT LOOK LIKE? | In verse 33, Jesus says, "But seek first the kingdom of God and His righteousness, and all these things will be added to you." What does it look like to seek His kingdom and His righteousness? Prayerfully and slowly marinate in the reality of the chart[1] below:

IN LIGHT OF MATTHEW 6:33

FALSE TREASURE	TRUE TREASURE
Pleasure	Knowing and Loving God
Recognition of People	Resting in God's Approval
Popularity	Servanthood
Wealth and Status	Integrity and Character
Power	Humility
↓	↓
Emptiness	Fulfillment
Delusion	Reality
Foolishness	Wisdom

It will take great courage in our age of consumerism and materialism to seek Jesus as the true treasure. In Christ's power, be courageous.

YOU CAN TRUST HIM | Seek God, the true treasure, and His righteousness. He will provide for your needs. Back in 1999 when my wife and I started One Heart at a Time Ministries, we had no idea how we would make a living starting a ministry. We were brand new Christ-followers. But we did read Matthew 6:33. When my wife and I decided that Matthew 6:33 was true, we started One Heart. And to our surprise, that very same day one of my neighbors wrote me a $2,000 check for the new ministry. I wept like a little baby in the middle of the street. And then the next day, my other neighbor did the same thing! Now, I am not saying that God is going to have your neighbors give you money, but I am saying He will meet your needs when you seek Him above all. I do not know exactly how He will do it, but He will.

Just recently, I had our church pray for a financial need that we were experiencing. Two days later, an unknown man who had heard me speak in the past wrote me a $200,000 check for our church. I cried again. God will provide for your needs so you can meet the needs of others. Through this gracious gift, we were able to use a significant portion to plant our first church and provide for people in need.

LEARNING TO BE CONTENT | When we treasure Jesus above all, God will adjust our needs according to His provision. Listen to Paul:

> Not that I am speaking of being in need, for I have learned in whatever situation I am to be content. I know how to be brought low, and I know how to abound. In any and every circumstance, I have learned the secret of facing plenty and hunger, abundance and need. I can do all things through him who strengthens me (Philippians 4:11–13 ESV).

Because of Jesus in you, you can weather any storm. He will strengthen you. Will this be easy? No. But He is trustworthy. Your trust in Jesus will be stretched. It will be troubling. Listen to Jesus in Matthew 6:34: "Therefore do not be anxious about tomorrow, for tomorrow will be anxious for itself.

Sufficient for the day is its own trouble" (ESV).

Let me leave you with this thought: What if the life you so desperately crave and the life the Great Hero hungers to give to you exists in the trouble that life drops on your doorstep? Hero-in-the-making, God's goal is not to spare you from trouble but to forge your character in the midst of trouble.

Seek His kingdom. He will provide.

HEAD

- Prayerfully reread Matthew 6:25–34.
- If you seek the kingdom of God and His righteousness first…God will meet your basic needs.

HEART

- What feelings are being stirred in you as you read today's entry? How have you been challenged or encouraged? Evaluate your life. Is there a decision you are facing? What would seeking His kingdom look like in that decision? What changes are you going to make through the Holy Spirit's power?

HANDS

- Develop a budget.
- Begin paying off your debt.
- Read Matthew 6:19–34 using *lectio divina* (entry 24).
- If you are not giving generously to your local church and those in need, start.

THIRTY-SIX

HERO, WORK HEROICALLY

Whatever you do, work heartily, as for the Lord and not for men,
knowing that from the Lord you will receive the inheritance
as your reward. You are serving the Lord Christ.

Colossians 3:23–24 esv

SACRED VOCATION | Coach D. W. Rutledge changed the course of my life.

A legend in the football-crazy state of Texas, Coach Rutledge has led seven Converse Judson High School football teams to 5A State Championship games, winning four in 1988, 1992, 1993, and 1995. He was named "Coach of the Year" seven times and "Coach of the Decade" for the 80s and 90s. In 2000, Coach Rutledge was presented with the prestigious Tom Landry Award, recognizing him as "a positive role model and a credit to the coaching profession." In 2003, he was inducted into the Texas High School Football Hall of Fame; in 2005, he was inducted into the Texas High School Coaches Association Hall of Honor.

Coach Rutledge is a great coach because he is a great man. He is a hero.

Coach was not just a coach…he was a father to many of us. The fatherly example that I went without at home was replaced with the fatherly example I saw in him. Even though we won a lot of games, he never talked about winning. Our motto, was "Do your best and don't sweat the rest." Coach was more concerned with our character formation as young men than just winning football games.

I asked him recently, "Did you know early on in your coaching career that you were creating a football dynasty?" Coach said, "I did not just want to be a successful coach. I wanted to be a significant coach by impacting the lives of the young men that God entrusted to me." Long after the high school games were over, Coach wanted his players to be successful men off the field.

Coach Rutledge has lived heroically and impacted young men because he knew that coaching was his ministry. Coaching was his sacred vocation. The word *vocation* means "calling." *Calling* means: what God has gifted you to do on earth to bring Him honor and you joy, for the good of others. Every Christ-follower has a sacred vocation. What is yours? And are you allowing the false division of the secular and the sacred to suffocate your calling?

ALL OF LIFE IS SACRED | For the student of Jesus, there is nothing you do that is secular (1 Corinthians 10:31). The word *secular* means "without God." Everywhere you go and everything you do is in and with our tri-personal God. The very God of the universe inhabits us. Therefore, the job you have is your sacred vocation. There is no such thing as the secular/sacred divide. One of the ways the enemy of your soul diminishes your imprint on eternity is by getting you to believe the lie that your job is secular and that church stuff is sacred.

THE LORD IS ONE | When the Bible proclaims that God is one (Deuteronomy 6:4; 1 Corinthians 8:6), it is not only proclaiming that there is only one God, but it is also proclaiming that the one true God is God over every aspect of your life. The hater of your soul wants you to live a fragmented life; God wants you to live a whole life. So when you go to work, God is going with you to empower and influence how you work. Your job is so much more than just a paycheck. You may hate your job now because you have yet to see it as your sacred vocation.

God has placed you in your sacred vocation to bring Him honor (1 Corinthians 10:31). The Great Hero has uniquely gifted you in your workplace to act with excellence and integrity. He has placed you there to be a humble servant in a culture that knows nothing of humility and servant leadership.

From 2003–2006, besides being a pastor and speaker, I was a guest football analyst for *Fox Charlotte TV*, and during the 2007 college football season I was a football analyst for *ESPNU*. I prayed just as much for God to empower me to do my TV job as I do to preach. If I work with humility and excellence and treat people justly, I bring honor, or fame, to God by respecting humanity and working hard. And we are most fulfilled when we, through the Holy Spirit's power, bring God fame.

———

There is freedom in knowing I can worship right where God has placed me. Living holistically, abiding in Christ in all that I do, allows the Great Hero to live through me and directs others to hopefully see Him in my life and therefore bring Him fame.

V. Gray

———

High school and college students—your schoolwork is your sacred vocation. God has given you a mind to cultivate and skills to enhance so you can maximize your potential and make Him famous through your life. Don't miss out on the opportunity to worship God in the midst of your education. All of life is sacred.

God has placed you in your sacred vocation to work as unto Him, not your boss (Colossians 3:23–24). When you go to work, you are not working for your boss. You are working as God's representative (Ephesians 6:5–8). Watch how your view of your job and your enjoyment of your job shifts when you see who your true Employer is. When I speak to NFL teams, I often tell the Christ-followers, "You should be the hardest workers on the team, because you are not playing for the team owner but for God's reputation!" Friends, your sacred vocation is for God, not man.

For those of you in positions of authority, one of the greatest ways you can represent God is by treating those under you with dignity, respect, and integrity (Ephesians 6:9; Colossians 4:1). Through your love for Jesus and His power resident in you, be Christ to them. Do not just work for success. Work for significance and impact their lives in a positive way. What would those who work for you say about your leadership?

God has given you your sacred vocation to provide for your family and those in need (2 Thessalonians 3:10). You have been gifted by God to provide for your family. A deep sense of accomplishment sweeps over me when my wife sends me a text saying, "Thank you for being a great provider." What an honor it is to be gifted to work. We are not only gifted to provide for our family's needs but also for the needs of the poor. Christ-followers, please keep in mind the poor as you work (Galatians 2:10).

YOUR VOCATION IS YOUR MINISTRY | The greatest missionary and ministry force in America is Christ-followers in the workplace. Please do not think you are not in ministry because you have a 9-to-5 job. The apostle Paul had what he called a "tent-making job," yet he saw Himself as a full-time missionary (Acts 18:3). Now, does this mean that you jump on a desk and yell, "Jesus is Lord!" with a 16-pound King James Bible? You can if you want to. I would not recommend it, though. I would recommend simply loving God and allowing His passion for people to become yours. As you do, God will arrange for conversations to take place as your coworkers see you working with excellence and serving those around you.

CONCLUDING THOUGHT | Coach Rutledge said, "Coaching is my ministry." He knew his sacred vocation. And he impacted lives...including the life of the man typing these words. Hero-in-the making, what is your sacred vocation? Whatever it is, get on with it and change some lives!

HEAD

- Prayerfully reread Colossians 3:23–24.
- Your vocation is sacred. Do not buy the lie of the secular/sacred split.

HEART

- What are you feeling as you read today's entry? How has this entry impacted your view of your job? What things in your job will change when you think of it as sacred? Write down your feelings and ask God the Holy Spirit to help you embrace the Jesus-forming work He wants to do in your life.

HANDS

- Who are the people that have impacted you in a positive way? Write them a letter of appreciation.
- Thank God for the job he has given you. Ask Him to help you work as He would have you represent Him.

THIRTY-SEVEN

HERO, SUFFER HEROICALLY

Consider it a sheer gift, friends, when tests and challenges come at you from all sides. You know that under pressure, your faith-life is forced into the open and shows its true colors. So don't try to get out of anything prematurely. Let it do its work so you become mature and well-developed, not deficient in any way.

JAMES 1:2–4 THE MESSAGE

THAT DAY | May 17, 2004, was the day I found out my bride and best friend had cancer.

This was not supposed to happen to a thirty-four-year-old former college track athlete who was in good shape and, as a registered dietitian, ate healthy food.

For about ten years Vicki had a small little knot on the upper part of the left side of her neck. We did not think it was a big deal until she turned to talk to the kids while driving and the knot moved. We made an appointment to see the doctor. He took some X-rays. Then he recommended that he surgically remove the knot. The surgery took two hours. As we would soon discover, the harmless knot was not so harmless after all.

On "that day," we walked into the doctor's office, waited for a few moments, then entered the room where we would find out the results. As the doctor entered the room, he uttered these words that still ring in my soul like it was yesterday, "You are not going to like this news. Vicki, you have Papillary Carcinoma" (thyroid cancer). In a matter of seconds, which felt more like forty years, I had several conversations:

First, the Great Hero and I conversed: "God, is this happening? Is my wife going to die?"

Second, as my bride and I clutched each other's hands, I tried as best as I could to look at her in a confident "Baby, everything is going to be okay" way.

Third, as I conversed with the doctor, I had to appear like a strong Christian who believed Jesus would take care of everything because I did not want to blow my opportunity to witness to him. I'm not too sure I pulled it off, though.

As we left the doctor's office, not a word was spoken. Just silence. Now that I look back, I think we were in shock. We got into the car. We both looked straight ahead with blank stares. After a few moments, I turned and looked at my bride and cried, "Not my baby."

SLEEPLESS IN CHARLOTTE | We tried to sleep that night. But that isn't going to happen when you know an alien killer named Cancer is trying to take your bride's life. As the night drifted on like a tiny rowboat in the roughest, darkest ocean, a light began to shine and break through the darkness…and peace began to still the stormy seas of our souls.

TENNIS | My bride, with tears streaming down her face, began to quote scripture to me. Then I began to quote scripture to her. She would say one. Then I would say one. This scriptural tennis match started slow…then began to pick up and get faster. Before we knew it, our tears of fear and sorrow had turned to tears of joy and hope.

That night laid the firm foundation as to how we would, in the Great Hero's power, fight for her life, capture this adversity, and use it to mature us as Christ-followers. We knew this battle would be great. But more importantly, we knew the Great Hero would fight our battle.

CHARACTER FORMATION | Disciples of Jesus: The Great Hero's goal for your life is not comfort, but character formation. One of the saddest things in life is not dying young, but living a long life and never really living at all. For the time that He has allocated for us here on earth, God's goal is to form in each of us the heart of Jesus. That's living. That's heroic. That is God's goal. He is so committed to His goal that God will use pain and suffering to accomplish this goal. I thank God for my mentor Alan Bacon, who taught us early on that suffering is one of God's most effective instruments in forming Jesus in His people. Listen to Romans 8:28–29:

> And we know that for those who love God all things work together for good, for those who are called according to his purpose. For those whom he foreknew he also predestined to be conformed to the image of his Son, in order that he might be he firstborn among many brothers (ESV).

I love this reality: For those of us that love Jesus, even the ugliness of suffering is used to forge us into the beautiful image of Jesus. In the midst of my wife going through two surgeries and having to be treated with radioactive materials to kill any remnants of the cancer, we had to learn how to embrace suffering as a gift.

Here's the deal: We are all going to suffer in life—so if we are going to have to go through it, let's suffer with the understanding that God is using it to make us more like Jesus. That's why we exist, isn't it?

Also, suffer in community. We experienced God's presence through God's people. The timely prayers and timely visits are gifts. When my wife had her second surgery, which lasted nearly six hours, no less than twenty people from our faith community came to the hospital to pray and be with me.

Every person on this planet will face suffering at some point. The question is, do we want to go through it with purpose? Lord, help me to rest in You so that when my loved ones are suffering, I see Your hand at work, trust You, and take the journey with them.

V. Gray

IT'S A GIFT | Was it easy knowing that my wife could die? No, it was the hardest experience of my life. I would have visions of my children and me overlooking a casket with my bride in it. Even as I write this, my eyes tear up and my heart feels like a knife just went through it. I love this woman only second to Jesus. It was hard then, and it is hard now.

But a strange thing began to happen as the shock of what was happening began to wear off. A supernatural peace enveloped us. Friends, that's the best I can explain it. We prayed like never before. We loved her like never before. We loved our children like never before, and I preached like never before. We became more patient and compassionate. In the midst of our great sadness, God surprised us with great joy. Like the Master Craftsman that He is, the Great Hero was making my wife and me more like Jesus. I now know from experience the words of James 1:2–4:

> Consider it a sheer gift, friends, when tests and challenges come at you from all sides. You know that under pressure, your faith-life is forced into the open and shows its true colors. So don't try to get out of anything prematurely. Let it do its work so you become mature and well-developed, not deficient in any way (THE MESSAGE).

As we suffer and respond in faith, trusting God to construct our lives in the image of Jesus, we develop into mature Christ-followers. And that's God's goal.

FIVE YEARS LATER | My bride is cancer-free. And we are more like Jesus. Has it been hard? Yes! Has it been worth it? Yes! If you want to live a heroic life, you must learn to suffer well, knowing that God is doing a great inner work in you.

My heart goes out to those of you who have lost loved ones. I watched cancer destroy my grandmother, the woman who raised me. It was gut-wrenching to see her die this way. Yet through the enabling hope and presence of Jesus, I had joy because I knew her suffering was over. More importantly, I knew that I would see her again in the new heaven and the new earth with a new resurrected body.

Let these words comfort you:

> Then I saw a new heaven and a new earth, for the first heaven and the first earth had passed away, and the sea was no more. And I saw the holy city, new Jerusalem, coming down out of heaven from God, prepared as a bride adorned for her husband. And I heard a loud voice from the

throne saying, "Behold, the dwelling place of God is with man. He will dwell with them, and they will be his people, and God himself will be with them as their God. He will wipe away every tear from their eyes, and death shall be no more, neither shall there be mourning, nor crying, nor pain anymore, for the former things have passed away." And he who was seated on the throne said, "Behold, I am making all things new." Also he said, "Write this down, for these words are trustworthy and true" (Revelation 21:1–5 ESV).

HEAD

- ❧ Prayerfully reread James 1:2–4 and Romans 8:28–29 using *lectio divina* (entry 24).
- ❧ God uses all things, including suffering, to conform you to the image of His son, Jesus.

HEART

- ❧ What feelings are you experiencing as you read today's entry? How has this entry impacted your view of pain and suffering? Write down your thoughts and feelings and ask God to empower you to work through them.

HANDS

- ❧ Write down one of the verses in this chapter and put it where you can see it daily until you memorize it.
- ❧ Write a letter to your younger self about a painful experience in your life. Tell yourself what you have learned through it. Consider sharing this with someone you know who is going through a difficult time.

THIRTY-EIGHT

HERO, DO SOMETHING ABOUT SUFFERING

Jesus...who for the joy that was set before him endured the cross, despising the shame, and is seated at the right hand of the throne of God.

HEBREWS 12:2 ESV

SAMMIE | Have you ever had an encounter with someone who forever tattoos your soul? God, in His providence, connected me with such a young lady from a small country town in North Carolina. Following my morning sermon at a summer youth camp, a brunette sixteen-year-old girl with sad eyes approached me and asked if I would talk with her at lunch. "Sammie" resonated with my message because I had mentioned that doubt and suffering were pathways of spiritual growth.

As we began to walk from the auditorium to the cafeteria across the dry soccer fields, she launched into a story of how she was beaten by her biological mother, sexually abused by her stepdad, and told by her biological father that she was worthless. Pause with me for a moment: I do not know about you, but it is painfully difficult to picture the hell that Sammie had gone through since the age of eight!

To cope with the ache that was embedded deep within her, she sliced up her arms with razors and even shoved nails into her ears. You may not understand that kind of pain, and I don't either.

As we connected over old hot dogs and corn that tasted like sawdust, I listened more than I talked. She taught me more than I could ever teach her. I listened to her story for about forty-five minutes...perhaps an hour. I wanted her to know that I cared enough just to listen; that she mattered to me. The more she poured out her fractured heart, the more fractured my heart became for her.

In this brokenhearted child, I experienced humility and spiritual authenticity; she embodied what it means to be honest with God. With a deep, piercing look into my eyes, she tenderly asked me, "Where was God when I was being beaten by my mom? Where was God when I was being sexually abused? Where is God now that I have been abandoned by my parents?"

People who have endured unexplainable suffering are often difficult to be around. They treat others as they have been treated—without respect. God, help me to see past people's faults and recognize their needs; to listen and love them right where they are.

V. Gray

Though she was from a small country town and spoke with a heavy Southern twang, she was intellectually sharp. She *knew* that the Fall of man had introduced sin into the world, leaving a wake of destruction in people like Hurricane Katrina left in New Orleans:

> You know the story of how Adam landed us in the dilemma we're in—first sin, then death, and no one exempt from either sin or death. That sin disturbed relations with God in everything and everyone (Romans 5:12 THE MESSAGE).

But what she had never *received* was the reality that Jesus had entered into her pain and experienced her hell during the Crucifixion. As best I could, I gently shared with her that our God is not absent from the hell we all experience on this journey called life; He is forever present in the mess we've made of this world. On the cross, Jesus became humanity's sin (2 Corinthians 5:21).

HE KNOWS | He knows what abuse feels like.

He knows what rejection and abandonment feels like.

He knows what having the hell beat out of you feels like.

As the entirety of humanity's sin fell on Him like an ax in the hands of an executioner, He experienced not only Sammie's pain but *all* the pain and suffering that would be birthed out of the womb of humanity's sin.

When it comes to suffering, no one has suffered as much as God. In the midst of our suffering, we often think that God does not know what we are going through. Actually, we do not know what God went through. God knows our pain—read Isaiah 53!

When it comes to the Resurrection, no one but Jesus could have pulled that off. He defeated death, pain, and suffering like the Great Hero that He is.

Where was God in the midst of Sammie's unthinkable torment? He was suffering and crying with her...but that's not all He was doing. He was also redeeming the wreckage of her life through His resurrection. Because He suffered and won, Sammie, too, can suffer and win through His life:

> I've told you all this so that trusting me you will be unshakable and assured, deeply at peace. In this godless world you will continue to experience difficulties. But take heart! I've conquered the world (John 16:33 THE MESSAGE).

> Therefore we do not lose heart. Though outwardly we are wasting away, yet inwardly we are being renewed day by day. For our light and momentary troubles are achieving for us an eternal glory that far outweighs them all. So we fix our eyes not on what is seen, but on what is unseen. For what is seen is temporary, but what is unseen is eternal (2 Corinthians 4:16–18 NIV).

HE HEALS | As our conversation continued, I could see the tender heart of a sixteen-year old girl begin to emerge from the grave. Sammie was honest as she said, "D. Gray, thank you for listening. I'm not a Christian, but you have helped me move a step closer to becoming one."

That night as I spoke to over 1,000 students, God the Holy Spirit revealed Jesus to her, the greatest treasure the human heart can possess and be possessed by. When, at the close of my sermon, I offered the students the opportunity to embrace Jesus as their God and to join His community called the Church, God the Holy Spirit called many teens to a life-giving relationship with Jesus. As I was walking offstage I took a quick glance back at the students that surrounded it. The last student I saw was the brunette sixteen year-old girl with a country twang, tears streaming down her face like a waterfall. May her tears be symbolic of God's healing grace falling upon her soul.

THE STORY IS NOT OVER | Two years later, as I began working on this book, I received an e-mail from Sammie. She is preparing to go to college. She wants to earn a degree in counseling so she can help girls who have gone through the suffering she has experienced. Sammie is a hero.

Until we reach the sin-free zone of the new heaven and the new earth (Revelation 21:1–4), there will be suffering and pain. The question is, will the Church respond in the Resurrection power of Jesus to do something about it, like Sammie? There are a lot of people who complain about evil and suffering and do nothing about it. Then there are people like Sammie who want to do something about it. She inspires me to be a hero. May she inspire you, too.

HEAD

- Prayerfully read Isaiah 53. Look at how Jesus suffered. He knows our pain.
- Through His Resurrection power, you, too, can overcome suffering and do something about it.

HEART

- What feelings are being stirred in you as you read today's entry? How has this impacted your view of suffering? Write down your feelings and ask God the Holy Spirit to help you embrace the Jesus-forming work He wants to do in your life.

HANDS

- If you have experienced great suffering and have unresolved questions, seek the care of a competent Christian counselor or minister to help you.
- Listen to someone tell you his or her story. It's a tremendous gift to give another person. Don't fix anything. Don't judge. Just listen and pray.

THIRTY-NINE

HERO, PORN WILL DESTROY YOU AND THOSE YOU LOVE

There's more to sex than mere skin on skin. Sex is as much spiritual mystery as physical fact. As written in Scripture, "The two become one." Since we want to become spiritually one with the Master, we must not pursue the kind of sex that avoids commitment and intimacy, leaving us more lonely than ever—the kind of scx that can never "become one." There is a sense in which sexual sins are different from all others. In sexual sin we violate the sacredness of our own bodies, these bodies that were made for God-given and God-modeled love, for "becoming one" with another. Or didn't you realize that your body is a sacred place, the place of the Holy Spirit? Don't you see that you can't live however you please, squandering what God paid such a high price for? The physical part of you is not some piece of property belonging to the spiritual part of you. God owns the whole works. So let people see God in and through your body.

1 CORINTHIANS 6:18–20 THE MESSAGE

READ THESE WORDS | Pornography is a wild beast that is devouring men and their families. I want you to reflect deeply on the words of a woman I know, whose life has been wrecked by pornography because her husband became consumed by this toxic poison. Here's her story:

> I began to sense the initial awe, the steady love, and the delightful excitement over me had fully evaporated.... Mean, spiteful, hurtful things came out of his mouth, sometimes with no rational explanation. He seemed incapable of recognizing how his insensitivity wounded me again and again. I kept forgiving, kept loving, kept trying to find a way past this ever-widening chasm. I wanted desperately to believe the man

I had grown to love—the godly, funny, kind, sensitive man—could be found again. This indifferent, cruel creature would hunt for my soft spots only to plunge another sword. I was increasingly compared to other women and found lacking.... Pornography isn't just about the women who are exploited in the making of it, although I have wept for them, too. It's not just about the men who are taken over and transformed by it. It doesn't stop with the women in those men's lives. The damage goes on to many other relationships.

MEN'S RETREAT | Awhile back, I was speaking at a men's retreat. After the third session, I sensed that God wanted me to tackle the issue of pornography head-on. After preaching, I placed a chair in the center of the room for the men to come and confess and receive prayer if they were struggling with porn. I sat in amazement of God's grace as man after man came forward to confess his porn struggles. I have seen boys as young as eleven and men as old as seventy confess during these times of restoration.

Porn addiction is so bad that *40 percent of pastors* have acknowledged visiting porn sites and *47 percent of Christians* say it is a major problem in their homes.[1] It is time for an all-out war against porn. Are you tired of being a slave to porn? Never forget this: God will rescue you from an enemy, not a friend. Is porn your enemy or your friend?

In a sex-saturated society, am I teaching my kids to view physical intimacy in a God-honoring way? I want to teach my children that their bodies are temples of the Holy Spirit, first and foremost; then all their decisions—what to do or not do—will be easier to make.

V. Gray

Perhaps you were like I was. In high school, watching porn was "normal." Little did I know that it would take years of God's grace and "reconstructive surgery of my soul" to set me free. Porn takes God's beautiful, mysterious gift of sexual intimacy and devalues it by making it shallow and ugly.

ADDICTION | Every time you watch porn, you are poisoning your brain with "erototoxins." According to sex education expert Dr. Judith Reisman:

> Thanks to the latest advances in neuroscience, we now know that pornographic visual images imprint and alter the brain, triggering an instant, involuntary, but lasting, biochemical memory trail.... Pornography triggers myriad kinds of internal, natural drugs that mimic the "high" from a street drug. Addiction to pornography is addiction to what I dub *erototoxins*—mind-altering drugs produced by the viewer's brain.[2]

There are fewer things more painful and heartrending than seeing a marriage wounded or even destroyed by pornography.

I have a friend who started watching porn while he was in high school. He was a good Christian guy, and no one knew his little secret except God. Even after getting married, he continued to view porn. At church, he developed into a leader of men—men looked up to him as he helped them learn to live the Christian life.

On the outside he was a model Christian; yet he had a dirty, nasty porn addiction eating away at his soul like a maggot. This man is one of my best friends, and he would occasionally travel with me and we often met to encourage each other in the faith. Even still, I wasn't aware of his addiction.

Instead of allowing God to help him with troubling issues like stress at work, feelings of inadequacy, or arguments with his wife, he would retreat and watch porn to *fix* himself. By viewing porn, the problems or stresses would ease for a while, as he would find temporary comfort. This cycle led to shame, guilt, and greater feelings of inadequacy.

One night at dinner, his wife, a godly woman who is sensitive to God's Spirit, asked him if he was viewing porn. He came clean and said, "Yes." For fifteen years my friend was addicted to porn; he lived in a prison of deception, disgrace, and remorse. And the more he viewed porn, the more guilt, shame, and deception were added to his life, which caused him to do it more! Do you see the downward spiral into darkness, despair, and pain?

My friend is now receiving help for his addiction. God's grace is healing him and his family; yet it is a very painful healing process. One day, my friend dropped his son off at school, and as he watched his boy walk into the building, emotions he had never felt before rose up in his heart like a tidal wave and tears filled his eyes. This newfound intimacy with his son was a result of being sexually pure. Porn no longer clouded his capacity to live and love.

Do I view sex the way God does, or have I allowed our culture to influence my views? Have I allowed the Lord to heal past sexual wounds so that they do not affect the physical intimacy I share with my spouse?

V. Gray

A WORD TO THE LADIES | Pornography is no longer just a man's issue. In recent years, more women have become viewers of porn. Ladies, if you watch this junk, you potentially will begin to devalue yourself and act out on what you see in porn films to find acceptance and significance. If you have journeyed down this road that is filled with despair, there is hope. It is found in Jesus. His love...His grace...His presence is only a request away. Through His unceasing mercy and forgiveness, He will reclaim your sexuality and empower you to worship the Great Hero through your sexuality as it was meant to be. Marinate in the Great Hero's promise to you:

> For you, O Lord, are good and forgiving, abounding in steadfast love to all who call upon you (Psalm 86:5 ESV).

FREEDOM IS NOT FREE; YOU MUST FIGHT FOR IT! | If you want to be free from porn, you must fight for your life. But you must fight in God's strength. Here are some practical steps that you can take to get set free from the grip of porn addiction.

First, admit your addiction to God. Stop hiding...He knows. And He loves you enough to forgive you and strengthen you so that you can escape porn's evil grip. This process will not be easy, but it will be worth it.

Second, confess your addiction to a group of men (or if you are female, to a group of women). It is vital that you have a community of people that will encourage, challenge, and help you get to the root of why you are addicted to porn. Professional counseling may be needed, too. These people who "do life" with you can hold you accountable to glorify God with your life. Remember: God's power is in you! You can do it!

Third, I suggest downloading XXXChurch's accountability software, X3watch. This free software will help you with online integrity. Whenever you are surfing the cyber-waves and access a site that may contain questionable (pornographic) material, the program will save the questionable site on your computer. Once or twice a month, depending on what you choose, your predetermined accountability partners will receive an email containing all the questionable sites you visited.

Church, it's time that we, by God's power, live heroically and kill this wild beast!

HEAD

- Reread 1 Corinthians 6:18–20. You are a temple of the Holy Spirit and you are sacred.
- Through the Great Hero's power, you can defeat porn.

HEART

- What feelings are you experiencing as you read today's entry? Why do you think you access porn? What emotions are you feeling immediately before you turn on the computer or television? Are you stressed? Sad? Mad? Identify these triggers. Write down your feelings and ask God to empower you to work through them.

HANDS

- If you are dabbling in or addicted to porn, confess it to God and godly people who can encourage you through this battle.
- If you are addicted to or dabbling in porn, list the ways it has negatively impacted you and your loved ones.
- Seek counseling if you need to.

FORTY

HERO, DANCE TO THE RHYTHM OF GOD'S GRACE

*But you will receive power when the Holy Spirit has come upon you,
and you will be my witnesses in Jerusalem and in all Judea and Samaria,
and to the end of the earth.*

Acts 1:8 ESV

DANCE | I come from a family of great dancers.

My grandmother could dance.

My momma could dance.

And I can dance.

In junior high school, if I wanted to go to the mall I was given enough money for bus fare. If I wanted to eat at the mall, I had to earn some money. The way I earned money was by break dancing. I would do a few moves, and people would give me a few bucks. It was fun.

There is a special something about great dancers that attract people. Think of the "Godfather of Soul" James Brown, the mesmerizing Michael Jackson, the super smooth Justin Timberlake, and the incomparable Fred Astaire. When we see great dancers, they give us a desire to dance, too.

Did you know that evangelism, or sharing the Good News of Jesus, is similar to dancing?

JUST DANCE | When I teach people how to share their faith, I teach what I call "Dancing to the Rhythm of God's Grace." Perhaps this illustration will help before I unpack this way of life. I've got some "old school" music on my iPod that I listen to. Sometimes, as I am writing or studying at the coffee shop while listening to it, I will start dancing. The rhythm will captivate me…it compels me to move…it stirs my soul. Within a few moments, someone will ask me, "What are you listening to?" I will simply remove my headphones and place them on the person. The same rhythm that moved me to dance begins to move them to dance.

Friends, the Holy Spirit is the headphones that allow you to hear the rhythm of God's grace. And as you begin day by day to dance the dance of love, forgiveness, justice, integrity, compassion, and courage, those in your sphere of influence will ask, "What are you listening to?" As your life is immersed in Jesus and His life is immersed in you, the "Jesus way of life" will burst forth from you, and as it does, people will want to dance like you are dancing—or at least want to know why you are dancing the way you are. When you are dancing to the rhythm of God's grace, you are inviting others to get down with God, too.

Evangelism is not something you do; it is someone you are. You are always evangelizing with your life. The way you treat people, the way you carry yourself at work, the way you parent, the way you treat the opposite sex, how you respond to adversity—just as all of life is worship, it is also evangelism.

————

When I seek after the Great Hero, letting Him live through me, He is drawing people to Himself through my life. I don't have to do—I can just be. As I love the people God has placed around me, doing life with them, my hope is they see Him in me.

————

V. Gray

The question is this: Are you dancing in such a way that your life invites others to get down with God, too? Or does your life make people not want to dance with God? The church in America is declining rapidly. One of the reasons is hypocrisy. Non-Christians are tired of us talking about our faith and not living our faith. They are tired of us talking and not dancing.

Think of it this way: If I were trained by a dance instructor for several years yet every time I hit the dance floor I had no dance skills, who would want to hire the dance instructor who trained me? You get the idea. People do not expect perfection. They do expect progression. Somehow, the lives of Jesus' followers play a role in non-Christians becoming Christ-followers (John 17:20–21). Ultimately God is in control of the results, yet somehow we join Him in this mysterious process (1 Corinthians 3:6–9).

Where God has planted you is your dance floor. Are you dancing? And does your dancing compel others to want to learn your moves? Let your heart marinate in this: The Great Hero is singing over you!

> The Lord your God is in your midst, a mighty one who will save; he will rejoice over you with gladness; he will quiet you by his love; he will exult over you with loud singing (Zephaniah 3:17 ESV).

Dance! The Great Hero is rejoicing and singing over you! Dance! Let the people see you dancing!

IT'S A PROCESS | Most people think that when someone becomes a Christ-follower, it is a one-time event, whereas the Bible describes it more like a process. The Bible uses agricultural imagery to describe the process of evangelism (John 4:35–39). Think about it: Crops do not just happen. Reaping the harvest is the outcome of a long series of events that cannot be overlooked.

First, the soil must prepared. If the ground is not cleared and plowed, it will not be ready to receive the seed.

Second, the seed is scattered over the field.

Third, cultivation of the seed must happen. This is the longest part of the agricultural process. It involves irrigation, fertilization, and weed control.

And fourth, only when the crop is mature is it ready to be harvested.

Now, replace the word *soil* with *soul*. A soul must be prepared, seeded, cultivated, and, only when it is ready, harvested. Many non-Christians are turned off by Christ-followers who try to harvest before the hard work of preparing, seeding, and cultivating has taken place.

I have watched my wife over the last eleven years live out the evangelism process. Through prayer (Colossians 4:2–6), being present in our neighbors' lives and available in times of need, and through answering questions about faith in Jesus, several women in our neighborhood have embraced Jesus and become His followers.

She's a great dancer. And others want to learn her moves.

To illustrate my point, I'd like to share Jeff's story with you.

JEFF | Jeff grew up in a somewhat religious home. Any remnants of religion were lost during his military years. After his military career, Jeff started a personal training business. One of our neighbors was one of Jeff's clients. For several years, our friend was preparing, seeding, and cultivating Jeff's soul. Jeff asked our friend some hard questions concerning faith in Jesus, so she recommended that Jeff meet with me to discuss those tough questions.

Jeff and I met over some coffee. I thanked him for taking time to connect with me. I listened to him share his story. I was impressed with his honesty. I asked him if I could share my story. We talked for about two hours; then the meeting was over. He did not miraculously fall to his knees and proclaim "Jesus is Lord." But I did feel like our time was successful because I knew that evangelism was a process. Perhaps God used me to prepare his soul some more or water the seeds already buried in him. Jeff mentioned to our mutual friend, "Derwin is a nice guy. He did not try to pressure me or anything."

I did not hear from Jeff again…until two years later. During one of our worship gatherings for our church, Jeff showed up with tears in his eyes. He asked if I could speak with him outside. He tried to tell me what was going on, but the tears and emotions of his circumstances were overwhelming him. As he gathered himself, he looked at me and described how his life was falling apart all around him. Then he said, "My friends said I need God, so I thought of you."

Two weeks later Jeff embraced Jesus as his God, his Life, and his Forgiver. He is now a vital member of our faith community. I've had the privilege of mentoring him in his faith-walk the last year. And you know what? Jeff's turning into a pretty good dancer himself.

Hero, it's time to dance to the rhythm of God's grace!

May the words of Darrell Evans's song, "Fields of Grace," reflect your life:

There's a place where I love to run and play;
There's a place where I sing new songs of praise.
Dancin' with my Father God in fields of grace,
Dancin' with my Father God in fields of grace.

I love my Father, my Father loves me;
I dance for my Father, my Father sings over me.[1]

HEAD

- Read Acts 1:8, 1 Corinthians 3:6–9, and Colossians 4:2–6 using *lectio divina* (entry 24).
- As you dance to the rhythm of God's grace, you are inviting others to get down with God, too.

HEART

- What feelings are being stirred in you as you read today's entry? How has this entry impacted your view of evangelism? Write down your feelings and ask God the Holy Spirit to help you embrace the Jesus-forming work He wants to do in your life.

HANDS

- List the names of five people in your sphere of influence (at work, school, gym, neighborhood, or coffee shop) who are not Christ-followers and pray for an opportunity to share and *be* the Good News with them.
- In the middle section of the book, I have explained the gospel using my own style. Reread it and work on how to communicate the gospel in your own creative and unique way.

FORTY-ONE

HERO, GET READY FOR BATTLE

Finally, be strong in the Lord and in the strength of his might. Put on the whole armor of God, that you may be able to stand against the schemes of the devil.

EPHESIANS 6:10–11 ESV

GET READY FOR BATTLE | On game day in the NFL, my teammates and I would have a laid-back breakfast about 7:30 a.m. At 8:15 a.m. we would board a bus from the hotel where we were staying to go to the stadium. Once we got to the stadium, we located our lockers. And in our lockers was our battle armor: the helmet; the shoulder pads; the belt, knee pads, and thigh pads; and the football cleats. Not much laughter or joking around...it was battle time. In a matter of a few hours, football at its highest level was about to be played. We were modern-day gladiators.

We had to be sharp.

We had to be ready.

We had to have laser-like focus for battle.

It was a ritual, putting on our battle armor. We had a helmet to protect our heads. Shoulder pads to protect our shoulders and chest. A belt to keep our pants up. Thigh and knee pads to protect our legs. And specially-made football shoes called *cleats* to give us traction on the field. Without our protective equipment, we would not only lose the game...we'd get hurt, bad.

In the same vein, you must understand how much more you need to put on the full armor of God as you, along with all Christ-followers, wage war against Satan and his demons who want to distract and destroy you (John 10:10; 1 Peter 5:8).

We are in the midst of a great spiritual war. Eternity and the "right now" hangs in the balance. And many Christ-followers are getting disseminated by the forces of evil because they are not wearing the full armor of God.

Heroes are on the front lines of the battle.

Heroes wear the full armor of God.

Are you tired of getting kicked around by the forces of evil? Then put on your armor and go to war!

SCHEMES | As a member of the Indianapolis Colts and the Carolina Panthers, I spent up to forty hours per week with my team, preparing for the opponent. We studied everything about our opponent. We knew their favorite plays; we even knew where each player on the opposing team had gone to college and how fast they could run. We would take home DVDs to study at night so we could know their schemes.

Why did we spend all this time studying our opponent? So we could win the game! The better we knew our opponent, the more we could develop effective schemes to defeat them. Consider this: If NFL teams spend this much time developing schemes to defeat their opponents, how much time do you think Satan and his demons take to develop schemes to defeat you (Ephesians 6:10–13)? Evil forces study you, and based on your weaknesses, they develop schemes to shipwreck your faith—or, if you are non-Christian, to keep you from embracing Jesus and His life-giving gospel.

I am often distracted from the great spiritual battle by things that have no eternal significance, giving the enemy leverage in my life. But when I set my mind on the Great Hero, He equips me with His spiritual armor. Lord, empower me for the battle that lies before me.

V. Gray

But God, in His grace, has not left us defenseless to fight the evil one and his army of demons. He has given His Ecclesia the full armor of God so that we can not only protect ourselves but also invade enemy territory (Ephesians 6:13). Jesus is the Victor who calls us to stand on the battlefield that He won with His blood (Colossians 2:13–15)!

BELT OF TRUTH | If I played an NFL game without my belt, my pants would fall down during the game. I would then trip…and America would see more of me than they needed to. God has given us the belt of truth to keep our spiritual pants up as we battle evil forces (Ephesians 6:14). The Truth is Jesus (John 14:6). He is the victorious One who keeps you standing firm in the midst of the enemy's assault.

Many Christ-followers are constantly falling in battle because they are not living in a Jesus-centered and -empowered life. The more you fix your mind on your abiding relationship with Jesus—asking the Holy Spirit to make Jesus more than just a theological statement but also a life-giving reality—the more He will abide in you and you will overcome the forces of evil (1 John 2:14).

THE BREASTPLATE OF RIGHTEOUSNESS | I liked my shoulder pads because I used them as weapons to tackle the opponent. They also protected some of my vital organs. The breastplate of righteousness likewise protects vital spiritual organs that would otherwise be open to attack, and it can be used as a weapon against the forces of evil (Ephesians 6:14).

At the bloody cross of Jesus, in the greatest act of love the universe will ever see, Jesus exchanged your unrighteousness for His perfect righteousness (2 Corinthians 5:21; Philippians 3:7–10). When the Great Hero looks at you, He does not see you clothed in your unrighteousness, He sees you clothed in Jesus' perfect righteousness (Galatians 3:27).

The forces of evil always want you to doubt your righteousness in Christ. If they can do that, then you will diminish the work of Jesus and this will cause you to live a performance-based life of trying to impress God through your behavior. This leads to empty, lifeless, shallow religion. The forces of evil would love nothing more than for your life to be unheroic. Every time you affirm your righteousness in Jesus, you are punching Satan and his demons in the face. As you affirm Jesus righteousness as your own, His power pole-vaults you to living righteously (Titus 2:11–14; Romans 6:11–14).

At the moment of conversion, Jesus gives you His righteousness as a gift (Romans 3:24). Now by faith, and with a heart of appreciation, accept it and wear it into the battle.

THE SANDALS OF PEACE | It is impossible to play effectively in an NFL game without football shoes. A good pair of cleats allows traction so you can stand firm in the midst of a game. God has given you "shoes for your feet" so you can be ready to share the gospel of peace (Ephesians 6:15).

Many Christ-followers have simply taken off their shoes and do not pray for or look for opportunities to give away the gospel to our broken world. God through Paul says "Put on the readiness given by the gospel of peace" (Ephesians 6:15 ESV). This means you are to be ready for battle. You are to be ready to proclaim the gospel that leads to peace *with* God (Romans 5:1), the peace *of* God (Philippians 4:7), and peace with your neighbor (Ephesians 5:21). Evil forces do not want people to have this. This is why the world is a mess! Put on your shoes, and through His mighty strength, get in the battle and kick some demonic butt (Ephesians 6:10–11).

THE SHIELD OF FAITH | Roman soldiers used large oblong shields that interlocked and protected them from spears and the flaming arrows of their enemy. Jesus is our shield and protector who blocks the spiritual spears and flaming arrows of our enemy. When our trust is in Him, it is our life in Him that blocks the flaming arrows of the evil one. As we mature in our trust of Jesus, He increasingly becomes our hope and confidence.

When talking about battling evil forces, many people usually slip into one of these two extremes: Evil forces do not exist…or evil forces cause everything. The way to balance this is by setting our minds on Jesus, not evil forces. He is the object of our faith. His all-sufficient and marvelous life is our shield!

THE HELMET OF SALVATION | Can you imagine trying to play a football without a helmet? That would not be good. Even so, there have been some players that have forgotten their helmets in the locker room before the game. And there are many Christ-followers who have left the helmet of salvation in the spiritual locker room. They are getting hit so hard by evil forces that they are getting spiritual concussions.

Battle-ready disciples wear the helmet of salvation by saturating their minds in God's Word and in the Truth that Jesus is their life (Galatians 2:20). If evil forces seduce you into doubting who you are in Christ and keep you so busy that you cannot spend time renewing your mind in the truth of the Good News, they will greatly decrease your effectiveness.

If evil forces have your mind, they will have your heart—and if they have your heart and mind, they will have your actions. When you put on your helmet of salvation by looking to Jesus, He will have your mind, your heart, and your actions. This is heroic.

THE SWORD OF THE SPIRIT | The sword is an offensive weapon in the Christ-follower's armor (Ephesians 6:17). You are to be aggressive in this battle. As you stab evil forces with scripture, they will flee from you (James 4:7). Jesus in His humanity stabbed Satan with scripture in the wilderness (Matthew 4:1–11). Through the Holy Spirit's power and the power of the Word of God, we, too, can sever the head of the enemy with God's Word! Marinate in the thought of this: When you immerse yourself in the Word of God, you will defeat evil forces through the power of God, just like the Son of God did.

PRAYER | A prayer-less life is a powerless life.

Prayer is an offensive weapon that is available to every disciple of Jesus (Ephesians 6:18–19). Pray for yourself—and pray for God's people. We are in a spiritual battle.

And when you pray, pray big prayers about the things of God and His kingdom, not little prayers about you and your kingdom.

Hero, it's time to storm the gates of hell! Take no prisoners.

HEAD

- ❧ Read Ephesians 6:10–20 using *lectio divina* (entry 24).
- ❧ You are a warrior in the great spiritual battle.
- ❧ Put on the full armor of God and storm the gates of hell.

HEART

- ❧ What feelings are being ignited in you as you read today's entry? How has this entry impacted your view of spiritual warfare? Write down your feelings and ask God the Holy Spirit to help you embrace the Jesus-forming work He wants to do in your life.

HANDS

- ❧ Write Ephesians 6:10–20 in your PDA or on a note card and place it where you can see it every day.
- ❧ Affirm the truth of this text, and by faith in Jesus, put on the full armor of God and go to war.

FORTY-TWO

HERO, FINISH THE RACE

Do you not know that in a race all the runners run, but only one receives the prize? So run that you may obtain it.

1 CORINTHIANS 9:24 ESV

BARCELONA 1992 | In 1992, at the Barcelona Olympic summer games, I saw an act of courage, perseverance, and love that forever tattooed my soul. British 400-meter sprinter Derek Redmond was fulfilling his dream of representing his country in the Olympics. He had spent countless grueling hours preparing for this one moment in history.

Derek got off to a great start.

He was running strong.

Then it happened.

Time stood still.

Derek buckled in agony.

He tore his hamstring muscle.

His Olympic dream lay in ruins as he collapsed to one knee.

Derek wept. I'm sure the pain of his injury caused him to cry. But I think the pain of not being able to finish the race hurt even more.

This next scene still brings tears to my eyes. Despite a torn hamstring, Derek rose to his feet and began to hop on one leg...he still has nearly 200 meters left. You can see the pain in his face and hurt in his eyes, yet he refuses to give in; he refuses to quit. He's going to finish the race!

All the other runners have long been finished.

With an unrelenting desire, Derek continues.

No matter how bad the pain, he continues.

As Derek, through sheer will and courage, continues, his father, Jim, runs out of the stands and eludes security guards to get to his son.

Jim later said to a reporter, "I wasn't going to be stopped by anyone."

As the security guards unsuccessfully tried to stop Derek's dad, he waved them away saying, "That's my son."

When Jim reached Derek, he said the words that I am sure comforted him since he was a little boy, "I'm here, son…we will finish together."

Derek buried his face in his father's chest.

They embraced.

Together, father and son finished what they had started a long time ago.

This story moves me in a much different way today than it did 1992. In 1992, I was twenty-one years old without a son. Today I'm thirty-eight with a son. This story of courage, perseverance, and love hits me with the G-force of a superjet.

I have coached my son's football team for three years. I've been training him since he could crawl. Football is in his DNA. He's a competitor. It is as if God has created him to be an athlete. Big Bull, as I affectionately call him, is also one of my best friends. He loves me and I love him. Mark my words: I would have done the same thing that Jim Redmond did for his son, Derek. If I ever see my son struggling in the battlefield of life, you best believe nothing and no one will stop me from getting to my son.

Let your soul marinate in this: If Jim Redmond, a human, would show this type of love for his son, how much more love do you think the Great Hero will show His sons and daughters as they run the race of life?

RUNNING THE RACE OF LIFE | Life is a race. And just like for Derek Redmond, there is a crowd of people watching how we run the race. All of humanity is born with a spiritual hamstring problem called sin that prevents us from running the race of life the way it should be run.

God sees our pain.

God enters our pain by jumping on the track of life and running with us and in us.

It is Jesus who carries us through to the finish line, which is the new heaven and the new earth (Revelation 21:1–4).

———————

My goal in life isn't to accomplish as much as I can, but to finish the race—and to finish well. God's Word defines that successful life: Love God with all your heart, soul, and mind; love your neighbor (Matthew 22:37–39); and introduce others to the Great Hero (Matthew 28:-18–20).

V. Gray

———————

BEFORE THE FINISH LINE | *Before we get to the finish line, many of our dreams will be shattered.* This can be a good thing. If Derek Redmond had won the gold medal, perhaps his name would not be known like it is now. As a result of his great response to adversity and the image of him and his father finishing the race together, that memory is forever etched in Olympic history. The shattering of your dreams could be just what you need so you can be the person God has created you to be.

Before we get to the finish line, we will need courage. The race of life is not for cowards! It's for courageous heroes! Being a hero does not mean that you never have fear. Being a hero means that in and through the resurrected Christ, you push through your fear in God's power to reach the finish line. Heroes take fear and use it as fuel to make them run faster!

Before we get to the finish line, we will need perseverance. I define *perseverance* as the God-enabled ability to keep our eyes on the finish line despite painful circumstances. The race of life is hard:

There will be a cancer diagnoses.

There will be pink slips.

There will be unspeakable tragedy.

But we persevere.

I have witnessed a lot of people who quit running because the race was too hard, too long, or required too much of a sacrifice. So they quit. You have not been created in the image of the Great Hero to be a quitter! In His mighty power, you can finish the race...no matter how hard, long, or great the sacrifice.

Before we get to the finish line, we must never, ever forget whose running the race with us and in us. Jesus is called Immanuel, which means "God with us" (Matthew 1:23 ESV). He is called the "Hope of glory," which is Jesus in us (Colossians 1:27). The Great Hero runs *with* you and *in* you to give you hope that you will experience glory now while you are running the race and ultimately when you cross the finish line.

So, run, Hero. Run. Run!

HEAD

- ❧ Read 1 Corinthians 9:24–27.
- ❧ Life is a race. The Great Hero is running with you and in you.
- ❧ Through Christ, run with courage and perseverance with the finish line in sight (Revelation 21:1–4).
- ❧ Jesus is running in you and with you (Matthew 1:23; Colossians 1:27). The Holy Spirit is in you (1 Corinthians 6:19–20). God the Father is in you (John 14:23).

HEART

- ❧ What feelings are you experiencing as you read today's entry? Write them down and ask God the Holy Spirit to help you embrace the Jesus-forming work He wants to do in your life.

HANDS

- ❧ Watch a video of Derek Redmond on YouTube. If you have children, let them watch it with you.
- ❧ Training is easier when you have running partners. Pray and search for a community of running partners to run with you.
- ❧ Run!

HERO, MAY I PRAY FOR YOU?

Dear Hero,

I wish I knew each of your names so I could address this letter to you personally. Perhaps the Great Hero will grant us an opportunity to cross paths one day in a coffee shop, at a conference, or in an airport. Thank you for taking the time to read, interact, and experience the Great Hero with me.

This journey has been humbling, frustrating, soul-stretching, and awesome! It has been humbling in that I still can't believe God used a kid from the hood to write a book! I hated reading until I became a Christ-follower twelve years ago. It was frustrating because eight days before the manuscript was due, my computer was stolen while I was preaching at a conference in Atlanta. If it wasn't for my good friend Chris McGinn, who not only reviewed my manuscript, but saved a copy of it, I would not have made my deadline. (Thanks for saving my bacon Chris.) It was soul-stretching because God brought more out of me than I knew was in there. And it was awesome because I have had the honor of sharing life with you. Thank you so much.

If you have been reading this book and you are not a follower of Jesus, please know that He is calling your name. He wants to know you face-to-face. And you need to know Him face-to-face. He wants to give you life, love, and liberty from anything that prevents you from being a hero. He has invited you to receive His life as your own. He has invited you to become His disciple in His family of disciples called the *Ecclesia*. He has invited you to participate in His mission of loving our dysfunctional planet. His invitation to life is free; embrace it by faith (Ephesians 2:8–10).

If you have decided to follow Jesus recently, let a friend who follows Jesus know so he or she can help you get integrated into a local community of faith. Please write me or email me and let me know of your decision. And to my brothers and sisters who have been walking with Jesus for a while now, please contact me and let me know how this book has impacted your life, too. Thank you.

May the words written on these pages be like heavenly soul food that nourishes you so you can be a blessing to the world. The world needs heroes, and God is in the business of making heroes. Please let Him design you into the man or woman you were created to be. It will not be easy. It will not be quick. But it will be worth it.

The world needs heroes. And you can be that hero.

I've decided to pray for you the prayer that I pray most often for my family, myself, and the congregation that I copastor. Let the truth of Ephesians 3:14–21 touch the depths of your being:

> I bow my knees before the Father, from whom every family in heaven and on earth is named, that according to the riches of his glory he may grant you to be strengthened with power through his Spirit in your inner being, so that Christ may dwell in your hearts through faith—that you, being rooted and grounded in love, may have strength to comprehend with all the saints what is the breadth and length and height and depth, and to know the love of Christ that surpasses knowledge, that you may be filled with all the fullness of God. Now to him who is able to do far more abundantly than all that we ask or think, according to the power at work within us, to him be glory in the church and in Christ Jesus throughout all generations, forever and ever. Amen (ESV).

On Mission with the Great Hero,

Derwin

One Heart at a Time Ministries
P.O. Box 472292 • Charlotte, NC 28247
www.oneheartatatime.org

NOTES

SECTION ONE

ENTRY ONE

1. Norman L. Geisler and Frank Turek, *I Don't Have Enough Faith to Be an Atheist* (Wheaton, IL: Crossway Books, 2004), 109.

ENTRY FIVE

1. The Josephson Institute of Ethics' Report Card on the Ethics of American Youth, http://josephsoninstitute.org/pdf/ReportCard_press-release_2006-1015.pdf (Los Angeles, 2006).

2. Kenneth Boa, *The Perfect Leader* (Colorado Springs: Victor, 2006), 15.

ENTRY EIGHT

1. Kenneth Boa, *Conformed to His Image* (Grand Rapids, MI: Zondervan, 2001), 67.

ENTRY TEN

1. David G. Benner, *The Gift of Being Yourself* (Downers Grove, IL: IVP Books, 2004), 49.

2. A Jewish poem, "Haddamut," composed in Aramaic in 1050 by Jewish cantor Rabbi Meir Ben Isaac Nehorai, in Worms, Germany, and later found on the wall of a patient's room in an insane asylum after he had died in the late nineteenth century. It is assumed that during moments of sanity, the unknown patient had translated the words. Upon hearing this story, pastor and songwriter Frederick Lehman was moved by the poem and adapted the words into the third verse of a hymn he wrote in 1917 entitled "The Love of God."

3. Boa, *Conformed to His Image*, 35.

SECTION TWO

ENTRY THIRTEEN

1. Benner, *The Gift of Being Yourself*, 87-88.

ENTRY FOURTEEN

1. Boa, *Conformed to His Image*, 118.

ENTRY TWENTY

1. Timothy Keller, *The Prodigal God* (New York: Dutton, 2008), 19.

2. Ibid., 18.

3. Ibid., 22.

4. Scot McKnight, *The Jesus Creed,* 6th ed. (Brewster, MA: Paraclete Press, 2007), 29.

5. William Barclay, ed., *The Daily Study Bible Series: The Gospel of Luke*, rev. ed. Louisville, KY: Westminster John Knox Press, 2000), 205.

ENTRY TWENTY-TWO

1. Yose Ben Yoezer, a rabbi of the early Maccabean period (164 BCE to 63 BCE), possibly a disciple of Antigonus of Soko and a member of the ascetic group known as the Hasidæans, though neither is certain. He belonged to a priestly family.

ENTRY TWENTY-FOUR

1. Richard Foster and Kathryn A. Helmers, *Life with God* (San Francisco: HarperOne, 2008), 12–13.

ENTRY TWENTY-FIVE

1. William Lane Craig, *Hard Questions, Real Answers* (Wheaton, IL: Crossway Books, 2003), 47–49.

2. Norman L. Geisler and Ron Rhodes, *When Cultists Ask: A Popular Handbook on Cultic Misinterpretations.* (Grand Rapids, MI: Baker Books, 1997), 81.

SECTION THREE

ENTRY TWENTY-SIX

1. Norman L. Geisler, *Baker Encyclopedia of Christian Apologetics.* (Grand Rapids, MI: Baker Books, 1999), 610.

ENTRY TWENTY-SEVEN

1. Michael Frost and Alan Hirsch, *ReJesus* (Peabody, MA: Hendrickson, 2009), 31-32.

2. Mark Deymaz, *Building a Healthy Multiethnic Church* (San Francisco: Jossey-Bass, 2007), 4.

ENTRY THIRTY

1. Gary Chapman, *The Five Love Languages* (Chicago: Moody, 1992).

ENTRY THIRTY-TWO

1. Boa, *Conformed to His Image*, 235.

2. Josh Weidman, *Dad, If You Only Knew* (Sisters, OR: Multnomah, 2005).

ENTRY THIRTY-FOUR

1. Dennis Rainey, "How Do We Deal with Financial Difficulties?" *Family Life Magazine*, November 13, 2007, http://www.familylife.com/site/apps/nl/content3.asp?b=3584679&c=dnJHKLNnFoG&ct=4639673 (accessed June 12, 2009).

ENTRY THIRTY-FIVE

1. Boa, *Conformed to His Image*, 67.

ENTRY THIRTY-NINE

1. Ron Luce, *Battle Cry for a Generation* (Colorado Springs: NexGen, 2005), 88.

2. Ibid., 84–85.

ENTRY FORTY

1. Darrell Evans, "Fields of Grace," *All I Want Is You*, Compact Disc, 2003.